Emotional Wellbeing

This is an essential resource for educators working to support emotional wellbeing in children and young people. Written by the team behind the Emotional Literacy Support Assistant (ELSA) training programme, it provides practical suggestions that can be implemented straight away to make a positive difference in the life of the young person.

The second edition of this bestselling guide has been fully updated and includes a new chapter on resilience as well as additional material on recognising and dealing with anxiety and anger. The chapters give a clear overview of each topic underpinned by the latest research in educational psychology, descriptions of vulnerabilities as well as case studies and suggestions for practical activities. Topics include:

- self-esteem;
- friendship skills;
- social skills;
- therapeutic stories;
- dealing with loss and bereavement.

Designed for use with individuals, groups or whole classes, this will be vital reading for ELSA trainees as well as anyone wanting to provide the best possible support for the emotional wellbeing of the young people they work with.

Dr Gillian Shotton works as an Educational Psychologist in Northumberland with a specialist remit for working with the children's homes and facilitating the ELSA programme. She is a field work tutor for the Newcastle University doctoral course in Educational Psychology.

Sheila Burton is the founder of the ELSA projects and has worked as an Area Principal Educational Psychologist in Hampshire. She is the author of the ELSA Trainers' Manual and she is actively involved in the ELSA network.

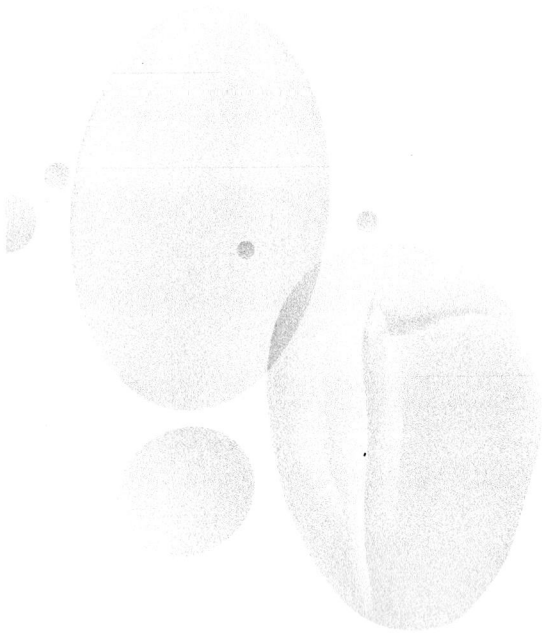

Emotional Wellbeing: An Introductory Handbook for Schools

Second edition

Gillian Shotton and Sheila Burton

Illustrated by Adele Agar

Routledge
Taylor & Francis Group

LONDON AND NEW YORK

Second edition published 2019
by Routledge
2 Park Square, Milton Park, Abingdon, Oxon, OX14 4RN

and by Routledge
711 Third Avenue, New York, NY 10017

Routledge is an imprint of the Taylor & Francis Group, an informa business

First edition published by Speechmark 2005

British Library Cataloguing-in-Publication Data
A catalogue record for this book is available from the British Library

Library of Congress Cataloging-in-Publication Data
Names: Shotton, Gillian editor.
Title: Emotional wellbeing: an introductory handbook for schools /
Gillian Shotton and Sheila Burton.
Description: Second edition. | New York: Routledge, 2018. |
"First edition published by Speechmark 2005"—T.p. verso. |
Includes bibliographical references.
Identifiers: LCCN 2018003027 (print) | LCCN 2018026719 (ebook) |
ISBN 9781315098463 (ebook) | ISBN 9781138298705 (Paperback) |
Subjects: LCSH: Affective education. | Emotions in children. | Educational
psychology. | Social skills in children. | Social skills—Study and teaching.
Classification: LCC LB1072 (ebook) | LCC LB1072 .E58 2018 (print) |
DDC 370.15/34—dc23
LC record available at https://lccn.loc.gov/2018003027

ISBN: 978-1-138-29870-5 (pbk)
ISBN: 978-1-315-09846-3 (ebk)

Typeset in Century
by codeMantra

Contents

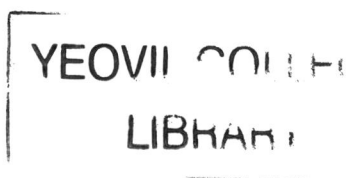

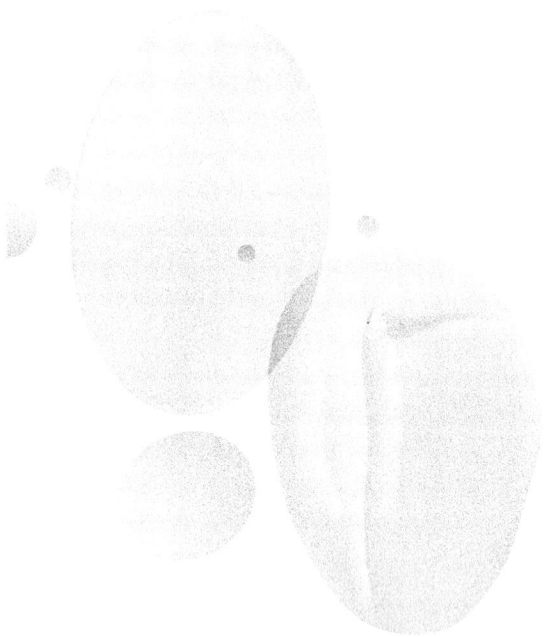

1. Introduction

In the last 30 or so years we have seen a strong government-led focus on raising pupils' levels of attainment, with schools being placed in league tables based on test results. For a time, this seemed to cause a narrow focus on academic achievement, with teachers feeling there was no time to be concerned about wider aspects of children's lives. Yet experience suggests that children learn better when their emotional needs are being met. As adults, we know that when we are faced with serious life issues like bereavement, relationship difficulties or financial stress it is harder to concentrate on our work and other daily responsibilities. Anxiety, fear and sadness are intrusive feelings that can incapacitate our ability to absorb information or learn new skills. Despite this we have sometimes shown a naïve expectation that children will come to school ready to learn.

As we entered the 21st century, central government initiatives focused more broadly on children's wellbeing. The Children Act 2004 (Every Child Matters) emphasised five priority outcomes for children:

- Be healthy

- Stay safe

- Enjoy and achieve

- Make a positive contribution

- Achieve economic wellbeing.

The National Healthy Schools Programme had from 1998 already recognised the important contribution schools make to children's general wellbeing, including emotional health. As part of the Primary National Strategy a suggested emotional literacy curriculum covering school years R to 6 was published by the Department for Education and Skills in 2005. Entitled 'Social and Emotional Aspects of Learning' (SEAL), it incorporated activities and supporting materials to enable class teachers to cover key topics in a developmental way year on year.

Changes of government led to changed priorities and the emphasis once more was narrowed to academic achievement. However, with increasing economic pressures following the global financial crash of 2008 and subsequent austerity measures, aimed at reducing the annual budget deficit, there then arose mounting concern over deteriorating mental health statistics for children and young people. Children and Adolescent Mental Health Services faced a crisis in funding. A growing number of children are receiving diagnoses of 'neurodevelopmental disorders', particularly autism and attention deficit hyperactivity disorder, and it seems the scarce resources are focused much more heavily on diagnosis rather than treatment. Schools have looked to health services to intervene, yet in many places they are offering very little more than pharmaceutical intervention. There is a scarcity of therapeutic intervention beyond drug therapies.

By necessity, the focus has moved to school-based intervention such as school counselling, parenting support provided by school-based staff, and emotional wellbeing support for pupils, delivered by school staff such as learning mentors and emotional literacy support assistants (ELSAs). The rapidly growing ELSA work will be discussed more fully in a subsequent section of this introduction. It was out of this work that the first edition of 'Emotional Wellbeing: an introductory handbook' was written to support those staff in schools that provide support to emotionally vulnerable children. A decade on, this second edition entitled 'Emotional Wellbeing: an introductory handbook for schools' expands upon the original publication with many new sections. It reflects additions to the original ELSA training which have been widely implemented by educational psychology services that provide this training and supervision programme to schools. The content is applicable to all kinds of school professionals that support vulnerable children and adolescents, as well as to those working with them outside the school environment.

Maslow's hierarchy of needs

One of the most popular and often quoted theories of human motivation was developed by Abraham Maslow and first published in 1943. He looked at motivation within the context of a *hierarchy of human needs*. Initially Maslow identified five levels of need.

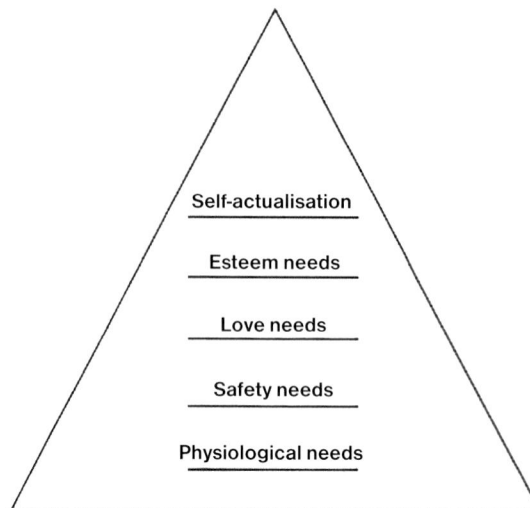

(Maslow 1943)

He referred to the lower four levels as deficiency needs which must be satisfied before we can act unselfishly. When they are met, higher needs emerge and become the focus of interest. When, however, we experience stressful conditions, or find ourselves under threat, we regress to a lower need level.

Physiological needs

Our most basic level of need is for air, water, food and sleep. If these needs are not met we may experience irritation, discomfort, pain or sickness. Such feelings motivate us to establish what is known as homeostasis – a state of balance where the needs have been satisfied. Once these basic deficiencies are alleviated we are able to think about higher level needs.

Safety needs

At the next level our concern is to establish stability and consistency in our personal world. We need to feel safe, not only physically but also psychologically.

Love needs

We all have the need to be loved and to receive affection from others. We are social beings and our sense of identity comes partly from belonging to a group. We therefore need to experience the acceptance of others.

Esteem needs

Esteem needs fall into two categories – self-esteem and esteem from others. The former arises from feelings of competency as well as specific achievements. The latter relates to our need to be appreciated and admired. It is more than just being accepted within a group; we desire the approval and affirmation of others. The extent to which we perceive ourselves to be valued by others affects our sense of self worth.

Self-actualisation

Self-actualisation is not described by Maslow as a deficiency need but a being need. It is the desire to make the most of our potential and become everything we are capable of becoming.

Maslow later refined his hierarchy by adding three further levels (Maslow and Lowery 1998). Cognitive then aesthetic needs precede self-actualisation, which is followed by a higher level of self-transcendence.

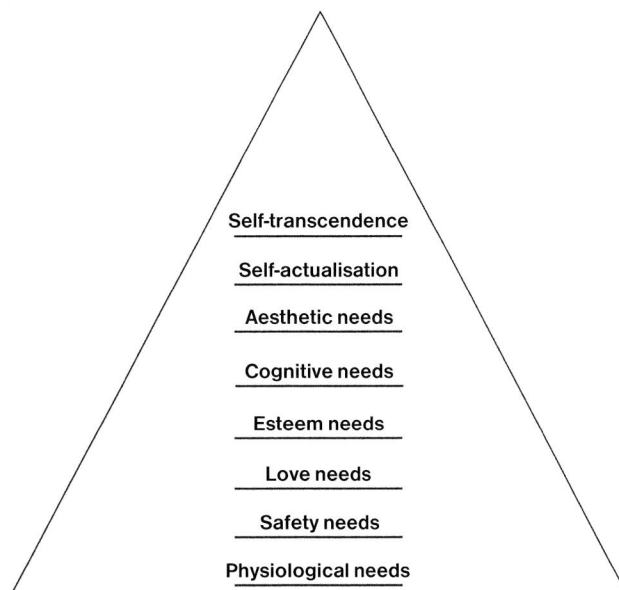

It is only when the deficiency needs are satisfied that we are motivated to seek knowledge for its own sake. We develop a desire for greater understanding of the world in which we live. Aesthetic needs are about appreciating symmetry, order and beauty within that world. The level of self-transcendence moves beyond personal fulfilment into a need to connect with something that exists beyond our self, or it may be about helping others to realise their potential. These needs may be considered to be a search for spiritual satisfaction.

Choice theory, developed by William Glasser (1998), shares much in common with Maslow's hierarchy of needs while also stating a need for fun and enjoyment. He rejects the psychology of external control for a psychology that focuses on sustaining the relationships that lead to healthy, productive lives. According to Glasser, almost all behavior is chosen, and we are driven by our genes to satisfy five basic needs: survival, love and belonging, power, freedom and fun. We choose all our actions and thoughts, and indirectly almost all our feelings and much of our physiology. He suggests that much of what goes on in our body is the indirect result of the actions and thoughts we choose. Glasser offers choice theory as a non-controlling psychology that gives the freedom to sustain relationships that lead to healthy, productive lives. Rather than blaming others for our behavior, choice theory invites us to accept personal responsibility for the choices we make.

Emotional literacy

Much is written these days about emotional intelligence or emotional literacy. Salovey and Mayer (1990) were the first psychologists to make a specific link between emotional and cognitive aspects of intelligence. In education the term emotional literacy tends to be preferred because it breaks away from the notion of a fixed, underlying level of intelligence that cannot be significantly altered. Emotional literacy, by contrast, can be nurtured and developed throughout life. Peter Sharp (2001) defined emotionally literate people as those who are *able to recognise, understand, handle and appropriately express their emotions*. We need to recognise the emotions we experience so that we can define them. As we develop an emotional vocabulary we are enabled to put our feelings into words. Without the language to communicate their feelings, children are reliant upon communicating through their behaviours. This may be through what we describe as 'acting out' behaviours, which present as overtly challenging and, if appropriate help is not provided, often lead to school exclusion. Other children, however, may become withdrawn in response to emotional distress; the greater risk for them is of their needs being overlooked because their behaviour is unthreatening to others. Emotional understanding is important if we are to learn from our experiences and develop resilience. Being able to manage our emotions allows us to build and maintain healthy relationships with others. As we learn to express our emotions in appropriate ways, we help both ourselves and other people, since an equally important aspect of emotional literacy is recognising, understanding and responding appropriately to the emotional states of others. These dual aspects may be referred to as *intrapersonal* skills (managing own emotions) and *interpersonal* skills (managing social interactions).

The importance of emotional wellbeing is receiving greater attention at all levels of education – government, local authority and school – and there are now many published books and resources, available through educational suppliers, that promote active support within school for children's emotional development.

There will always be some children in our schools whose ability to learn is adversely affected by emotional and psychological difficulties. If we give them the chance to think about these difficulties within the context of a relationship that is supportive and safe, we can help them become more resilient in the face of adversity. As they feel better able to recognise and manage their feelings, they will engage more readily with the learning challenges presented to them in school.

Gender differences

There are notable differences in the development of emotional literacy between the sexes. In *'The Essential Difference'* (2003), Simon Baron-Cohen reports how females on average develop faster than males in their ability to empathise. In contrast males develop faster than females in systematising (the ability to identify how a system or mechanism works and thus be able to control or predict its behaviour). He found that at one year old, girls make more eye contact than boys the same age. In fact he has discovered a link between the amount of prenatal testosterone by the foetus and later measures of sociability in the child. The higher the level of prenatal testosterone the less eye contact the child will make as a toddler. Baron-Cohen hypothesises that people with autism or Asperger's show an extreme form of the male profile in having significant difficulties with empathy alongside adequate or superior ability to systematise.

Some specific differences we might observe include:

- Females have been shown to have better language ability in general than males. It seems likely that good empathising would promote language development and vice versa, so these might not be independent (Baron-Cohen et al 1997).

- Girls from one year old show greater concern through more sad looks, sympathetic vocalisations and comforting (Hoffman 1977).

- Women's conversation involves much more talk about feelings, while men's conversation tends to be more object- or activity- focused (Tannen 1990).

- From birth females look longer at faces, particularly at people's eyes. Males are more likely to look at inanimate objects (Connellan et al, 2001).

- Women are better at decoding non-verbal communication, picking up subtle nuances from tone of voice or facial expression, or judging a person's character (Hall 1978).

- More women value the development of altruistic, reciprocal relationships, which by definition require empathising. In contrast, more men value power, politics and competition (Ahlgren and Johnson 1979).

Even expressed at normal levels, aggression can only occur with reduced empathising. Here again, there is a clear sex difference. Males tend to show far more 'direct' aggression (pushing, hitting, punching, etc.) whereas females tend to show more 'indirect' (or 'relational', covert) aggression (gossip, exclusion, bitchy remarks, etc.). Direct aggression might require an even lower level of empathy than indirect aggression. And indirect aggression needs better mind-reading skills than does direct aggression, because its impact is strategic (Crick and Grotpeter 1995).

Chaplin and Aldao (2013) conducted a review of 166 studies on gender differences in emotional expression from infancy through adolescence and considered possible moderators of those differences. They found significant but very small gender differences overall, with girls showing more positive emotions and internalising emotions (sadness, anxiety, sympathy) than boys, and boys showing more externalising emotions (e.g. anger) than girls. These gender differences were moderated by age, the interpersonal context (i.e. whether they were with parents, strange adults or peers) and the nature of the task in which they were involved.

This demonstrated the importance of contextual factors in gender difference. Gender differences in positive emotions were more pronounced with increasing age. Girls showed more positive emotions in middle childhood and adolescence. Boys showed more externalising emotions than girls at toddler/ preschool age and in middle childhood, but fewer externalising emotions than girls in adolescence. For positive emotions these gender differences were less pronounced when children were interacting with their parents and more pronounced with unfamiliar adults. For externalising emotions, the differences were more pronounced when children were with their peers or were alone. It is important to note that this study focused on emotional expression, not emotional regulation.

Gender differences are a complex area of research and there is likely to be an interaction between biological, cultural and contextual factors when looking at this topic. Also, it needs to be remembered that gender differences are trends and there will be many exceptions within the population to these general trends.

Emotional literacy support assistants (ELSAs)

When children have learning difficulties, they are provided with special programmes of support to enhance their academic learning. It is however, equally important for schools to recognise the need to plan additional support to address their emotional needs. This handbook has arisen out of work by the authors to train and assist emotional literacy support assistants (ELSAs) to work with children and adolescents, both individually and in small groups, on aspects of emotional literacy (Burton and Shotton 2004).

The ELSAs were initially trained to develop interventions in the following areas:

- Emotional awareness
- Anger management
- Self-esteem
- Social and communication skills
- Friendship skills.

Support for loss and bereavement issues has since become a core part of the training. Chapter 9 on loss and bereavement has been extended to look in greater detail at the losses experienced by children caught up in parental separation and divorce. Anger management training has been broadened to cover emotional regulation in general, including coping with anxiety. A growing number of children are presenting in school with high levels of anxiety. Without support, a significant number develop reduced and irregular school attendance, possibly missing out on years of education. Chapter 5 in this book has been extended to include the support of anxious pupils. The ELSA training on self-esteem has been broadened to include input on motivation and building competence, which is reflected in chapter 4 on self-esteem. Resilience, or the ability to recover from adverse life experiences is linked with self-esteem. There is a new chapter 10 in this latest edition of *Emotional Wellbeing* that explores the subject of resilience.

Their programmes of support, which typically would be delivered weekly for at least half a term, but in some cases for rather longer, are designed by ELSAs to meet the individual needs of the specific children with whom they work. It is important to recognise that the development of emotional literacy in children is facilitated rather than didactically taught. Indeed, learning is usually more effective when it is experiential. ELSAs are encouraged to use lively and interesting resources including games and puppets, rather than relying too heavily on worksheets. Encouraging pupils to talk is a key role of an ELSA. Feedback from children and young people themselves has shown that one of the things they most appreciate is having someone with the time to really listen to them. For some of them, it is their first experience of undivided adult attention.

Research

There is a growing body of research that suggests that the ELSA training, and support consequently given to pupils, has the following outcomes:

- Staff who receive the training have greater levels of self-efficacy; they are more likely to believe that they can make a difference in the lives of the children they work with. They feel more empowered and valued within their role in school (Grahamslaw 2010).

- Staff perceive a positive impact on behaviour, emotional wellbeing and peer relationships (Bravery and Harris 2009).

- Using the strengths and difficulties questionnaire, teachers' perceptions of the children's behaviour improved post intervention; prosocial behaviour increased and levels of peer problems and hyperactivity decreased (Burton, Osborne and Norgate 2010).

- ELSA support helped children to develop a sense of self and improve their resilience (Bravery and Harris 2009).

- Children valued specific strategies and practical activities in the sessions (Hills 2016).

- Pupils appreciated having someone to talk to in school who listened to them without criticising and showed them unconditional positive regard. Developing such a relationship with the ELSA helped the children to feel that they had an advocate within school (Hills 2016).

- Pupils also talked about the importance of being able to talk about their feelings, not bottling things up, which they said made them feel happier. They also spoke about being able to reframe situations and see things differently through ELSA support (Hills 2016).

Examples of quotes from pupils who have received ELSA support:

- *It makes me happy and feel good*

- *I've got better at listening*

- *I don't worry anymore*

- *I've learned how to play nicely.*

Teachers notice progress in most children that receive this kind of support. The kind of comments they make include:

- *She seems more confident in class – answering questions and leading others in a group task*

- *His behaviour is much improved and as a result his school work has improved*

- *She has recently made improvements in maths, which she finds difficult, due to gaining confidence*

- *He is much more settled, more focused and can control his behaviour better.*

In devising the ELSA initiative, it was always intended that, in addition to providing indirect support to vulnerable pupils, educational psychologists would build capacity in schools to address a wide range of emotional needs present in the school population. This would be achieved by empowering staff to develop their confidence and competence in offering support. The success of this approach is attested to in the following comments made by an ELSA in London:

> Being part of the ELSA project is an amazing experience. The training was intense, but it provided me with new found information about the importance of emotional literacy and the positive effects of the intervention. I feel very empowered as an ELSA; the experience has impacted my life not only professionally but personally as a parent and as an individual. As Aristotle comments, 'Educating the mind without educating the heart is no education at all.'

There is a website dedicated to the ELSA initiative – www.elsanetwork.org. It sets out the principles behind this work and shows how widespread the application of this intervention has become. As well as publicising this approach to developing emotional wellbeing in schools, it is designed to be an ongoing support both to ELSAs and to the educational psychologists who train and supervise them.

Building relationships and modelling appropriate skills

Promoting emotional wellbeing is not only about desirable skills to develop. It is also very much about the context in which that can happen. An approach of '*Do as I say, not as I do*' will get us nowhere. Children learn less by what they hear and more by what they see. We also know that they learn better when they feel safe. To offer children effective support we need to invest time in building quality relationships with them. The greatest secret of success within the ELSA programme is probably the time and skills invested in building a relationship of trust. Many of the children with whom ELSAs work have experienced failure and rejection over long periods of time. Some have never learned that it is safe to trust adults at all.

Emotional literacy is something that we model rather than teach. Indeed, if it can be taught at all it is taught through example. Unless children experience respectful caring relationships from others they will not know how to develop them for themselves, or even that these are something to aim for. We gain children's respect by giving respect.

If our desire is to help children cope with their feelings and behave in positive ways, then we need to work hard on our own coping strategies and interpersonal style. This means learning how to manage our own emotions well in the face of challenges, frustration and disappointments. Unless we can live according to the standards we espouse and be people that others would aspire to imitate, the things we say will lack credibility in children's eyes.

Those working with challenging and emotionally vulnerable youngsters must have a genuine desire to come alongside and make a difference. They need to be people who will befriend them in the sense of believing in them and truly caring for their wellbeing. Children are keenly aware of whether a teacher or support assistant likes them or not. Since the most powerful part of our communication is the non-verbal signals we give off, our real feelings towards others will always leak out.

Successful relationships with children require us to be child-centred. This is not about giving in and letting them do whatever they want. It is about the ability to see things from their perspective and offer understanding. Children need to know they count. Their feelings, however misconstrued, really matter.

About this book

Any emotional literacy curriculum will work towards helping children to make the link between feelings, thoughts and behaviour. How we are feeling affects our thinking, but it is also the case that what we are thinking affects the way we are feeling. Our thoughts and our feelings together have a strong impact on our behavioural reactions. If I think my best friend is ignoring me because she does not like me anymore I may feel hurt and become critical of her. If I think she has failed to notice me because she is engrossed in what she is doing, the impact will be less. I may feel mildly disappointed, but reason that I, too, am sometimes less aware of others when I am busy.

The scope of this book is to provide support to those school staff who work specifically with children to enhance their social and emotional coping skills. The topics of focus have been chosen because the authors see them as key areas of competence needed by children, so they might make the most of life's opportunities. Each chapter incorporates practical ideas for supporting children to increase their emotional literacy skills.

Chapter 2 – Keys to good communication: Some basic counselling skills are explained that are considered essential to building successful relationships between a helping adult and the child. A range of practical resources are suggested to incorporate into emotional literacy programmes of support, enriching the supporting adult's exploration of a pupil's emotional responses to their life experiences.

Chapter 3 – Recognising and managing feelings: While children can experience a full range of emotions they are often unable to identify them accurately. Naming the feelings starts to bring order to their emotions. Developing an emotional vocabulary enables children to tell us how they feel, and this can reduce the extent to which they need to act out or withdraw into those feelings. An extensive discussion of the brain physiology underlying emotional regulation is included in this chapter.

Chapter 4 – Self-esteem: Many children in our schools experience low self-esteem, especially if they find learning difficult or have weak peer relationships. They need help to recognise the skills they have and appreciate their unique personal value. Self-esteem is a multifaceted concept, so having difficulties in one aspect of self-esteem does not imply difficulties in all aspects. In this chapter we look at some different domains of self-esteem to help practitioners be more targeted in their work.

Chapter 5 – Working with uncomfortable emotions: Strong emotions can be difficult to handle, even for adults who have had years to practise! Some of the children we work with have not learned how to keep themselves or other people safe when they are frustrated and become angry. The assault cycle of emotional arousal is presented, and the firework model of anger is explained as a means of helping children understand this emotion better. An increasing number of children in school are experiencing levels of anxiety that impair their social and academic functioning. In this chapter the link between thoughts, feelings and behaviour is explored. Some practical strategies for managing both anger and anxiety are suggested.

Chapter 6 – Friendship skills: For most children friendships develop naturally. Others need help to learn how mutually supportive relationships are established and maintained. Some may even be unaware of their need for friends, and that without them they will miss out on the richness of learning that springs from special relationships built on shared interest and trust. There is extensive explanation of the Circle of Friends intervention and guidance on running friendship skills groups.

Chapter 7 – Therapeutic stories: This narrative approach is an invaluable way of helping children find hope and possible ways of coping with the difficulties they have. Because the stories are not explicitly about them, children's natural defensiveness about their own feelings and behaviour can be circumvented. By identifying with the experiences of the central characters, however, they come to realise that they are not alone in their difficulties and may be encouraged to find new approaches for themselves.

Chapter 8 – Social skills: The skills of social interaction do not come naturally to all children. They need to be modelled and sometimes overtly taught in order to help children relate effectively to adults and to the other children around them. We identify some key constituent skills for effective social interaction and present some ideas for developing these. Basic principles of writing social stories to help address social interaction difficulties are explained and there is a section in this chapter on using Lego construction tasks within small groups to improve children's social communication skills.

Chapter 9 – Supporting children through loss and bereavement: There are many kinds of loss experienced during life. The most challenging are the losses associated with relationship breakdowns in the family that lead to separation and divorce and those experienced through the death of a loved one. Several models of the grief process are described, and practical ideas given for supporting children to come to terms with the changes associated with loss, both through death and family break-up.

Chapter 10 – Resilience: Children vary considerably in their ability to recover from adversity. Resilience relies upon a complex interaction of factors including the nature, amount and frequency of the difficult challenges faced, together with the presence of internal and external protective factors. Internal protective factors include the ability to regulate emotional states effectively and the capacity to maintain a generally positive mindset. External protective factors include the presence of a caring relationship and positive school experiences.

2. Keys to good communication

Introduction

To enable children to be comfortable enough to contemplate change it is essential to create a climate of acceptance and easy communication. Successful social interaction requires us to have sufficient space in our mind for the other person so that we are able to offer full attention to what they bring to the conversation, both in the things they say and the way they are.

Conveying our availability is helped when we create a safe space where we can talk together without interruptions from others. Quality conversations are made easier in a comfortable environment in which both parties are enabled to feel relaxed and unhurried.

This chapter will explore some of the attitudes and skills that promote a therapeutic relationship between an adult and child, and will then consider some common barriers to open communication.

Being genuine and respectful

A good relationship is founded on genuineness. To work well with children we need to be at ease, without feeling the need to play a professional role when talking with them. They need to know we want to help because we care about their wellbeing, not simply because we are paid to do so. This requires us to believe that working with the child is worth our time and effort. We need the ability to be spontaneous yet not uncontrolled in our response towards them. If a child is upset we can show concern, but it will not help for us to burst into tears too! Similarly it is unhelpful to show ourselves horrified by things they share, as our alarm may lead them to become more reticent.

It is important to remain open and non-defensive towards them, even when we feel criticised by what they say and how they are behaving towards us, or when we feel uncomfortable about their criticism of someone else. Each child is unique and needs to be valued for who they are. A supportive and respectful relationship is built upon unconditional positive regard, which means looking beyond any difficult behaviour to a child expressing needs, however clumsily. We should always assume that they are good at heart. Maintaining a positive attitude towards them in the face of challenge gives a very powerful message of being valued despite their difficulties. Respect is about valuing others simply because they are fellow human beings. There also needs to be consistency between our declared values and our own behaviour. Our values may sometimes conflict with those of a child we are working with, yet it is possible to maintain our own values while remaining tactful and respectful towards them and their views. We don't have to approve of everything they do, but we need to respect their intrinsic value as a person.

Relationships are two-way, so in assisting a child to have the confidence to open up to us it can be helpful to share something of ourselves. This is referred to as self-disclosure and needs to be handled with sensitivity. We should hold in mind the question, 'Is this helpful to share?' It is important to remember that we are providing children with the opportunity to unburden to us, not the other way round! Too much self-disclosure can divert attention away from the child and their issues.

An important aspect of showing respect is to maintain confidentiality, within the accepted limits around child protection. It is important to avoid telling other people things that the child only wanted to share with us, providing that maintaining confidentiality does not put them at risk. If we consider it helpful to share information with another it is respectful to seek the child's agreement, explaining why we think it would be helpful for the other person to know.

Showing empathy

Empathy is about being able to relate to a child's feelings and communicate understanding. It involves seeing things from their perspective, sometimes referred to as putting ourselves into their shoes. This requires us to put our own experiences to one side and project ourselves into the experiences of a child, as if we were them. To do this requires imagination, while keeping a firm hold on our own reality. The 'as if' quality of empathy prevents us from being sucked into the other's emotions and becoming overwhelmed by their difficulties. Once that occurs we take on their helplessness and find ourselves unable to assist them.

Empathy is different from identification. 'Oh, I know just how you feel – exactly the same thing happened to me,' is a statement of identification rather than empathy, confusing our own experience with that of the child. We need to be able to keep our experience separate from theirs. Situations and our reactions to them may be similar but will never be identical. Confusing our respective experiences can lead us to lose sight of their issues and begin to focus on our own.

It is also different in quite a subtle way from sympathy, which is a reaction to the plight of the child – feeling sorry for them. An expression of sympathy may be entirely appropriate but we offer it while remaining separate from the child's experience. Empathy, by contrast, involves us imagining ourselves in their position. Sympathy can quickly be offered but it takes time to listen and understand another person's perspective without racing ahead to offer solutions. We show empathy by how well we listen and interpret, from verbal and non-verbal communications, what it is like to be that child at that time. This includes the feelings and hidden messages behind the behaviour.

Actively listening

Attentive listening is far from passive. Indeed, it requires a high level of concentration to attend fully to another, listening not only to what is said but noticing their tone of voice and body language. There is always a danger that we do not listen carefully to what a child is telling us because we have predicted what their message is about and are planning our response. This is especially so when a child is long-winded in their explanation and we are very conscious of time.

We are not always good at listening to a child's point of view if we sense it needs to be challenged. We are tempted to step in and correct some inaccuracy or faulty thinking before giving them the space to fully express their concerns. In this way we may inadvertently reinforce their perception that 'nobody listens to me'. In a helping relationship we need to remain alert to our own biases or prejudices, which may hinder us in hearing an alternative point of view.

Another challenge for us may be our own distractibility. We are often aware of how highly distractible some children are, yet our own attention can easily be drawn away to something else, including those tangential thoughts that pop into our minds about a task to be done or a message to be given. Those of us who strongly identify with this last point need to think about how we can help ourselves to remain more focused. Distracted thinking is well nigh impossible to hide! One of the key indicators of attentive listening is good eye contact. Trying to talk to someone who hardly looks at us is very disconcerting because we feel they are disinterested, and most of us will tend to dry up. (Some children are very uncomfortable giving eye contact, so encouraging them to focus on the end of the nose is a helpful strategy because it looks as if they are looking us in the eye.)

Elements of communication

It is easy to assume that the spoken word is the most important element in communication between two people. In the field of communication studies, however, it is recognised that the words themselves represent a very small proportion of the impact of a message. A considerably greater importance is placed on what is known as paralanguage – voice tone, inflection, pace and speed of speech. For a simple demonstration of this, try saying several times out loud the sentence, 'I didn't say she stole my purse,' each time putting the emphasis on a different word, and see how it changes the meaning. More important still, accounting perhaps for more than half the communicative value of the message, is body language – gesture, posture and movement. This may be one reason why some people are uncomfortable using the telephone, while the cumulative impact of body language with paralanguage suggests that emails, which are often written hurriedly, may be especially vulnerable to misinterpretation.

Non-verbal communication

In talking with children we need to be attuned not only to what they say, but to their whole demeanour. It is especially important in therapeutic conversations to notice any incongruence between what a child says and their non-verbal communication. While it will not always be appropriate to comment at the time, it could be addressed sensitively along the lines of, 'You say you don't care what he thinks of you, but I notice you are looking upset.' This gently invites the child to think further about the impact upon themselves of the circumstances they are recounting. Non-verbal communication will reflect true feelings when there is a contradiction with what is being said.

With this in mind, we need to recognise that the same is also true of us. If we feel impatience, scepticism or even plain dislike of the child, those feelings will certainly leak from us and undermine any work we try to do with them. Children are very good at seeing through us if we are only pretending to be positive.

Our body language has a powerful impact on the behaviour of the child talking. If we maintain an open and relaxed body position they are more likely to relax and open up with us. If we mirror their body language, without descending into mimicry, it communicates empathy. Looking interested in what they say to us reassures them in the telling of their story, encouraging them to persevere and tell those bits that may be hard for them to share.

Some useful verbal strategies

When we listen to someone tell their story the important elements may not always be clear to us. It is helpful to pause and clarify. Clarification may be by seeking additional information to help us understand better ('Can you tell me more about that?'), or it may be by checking that we have understood correctly ('Do you mean ...?').

To ensure the accuracy of our understanding it is helpful to summarise from time to time. It is a way of checking that we have heard what is important for the child and are not overlooking key information. A summary should be presented in a way that allows the child to correct any misunderstanding on our part ('So let me see if I've got this right; the thing that worries you most is ...'; I think the main points we've talked about today are ...').

The ability to reflect back what the child has said is an important skill. It shows that we have heard them, but may also bring them into greater awareness of their own thoughts and feelings. Sometimes this is done by repeating a key word or phrase, but making sure we avoid a questioning inflection (Child: 'He just doesn't care. I know he hates me.' Adult: 'Hates you.') Sometimes it is done by picking out the feeling behind the words ('It sounds like you are very upset.') Or it may be done by paraphrasing what the child has said (Child: 'I completely mucked it up.' Adult: 'You think you got it all wrong.').

Reflecting feelings enables a child to develop the language to describe their own emotions. We tentatively name these and check it out with them. Being able to articulate our emotions reduces the need to demonstrate them in less helpful ways – a theme developed more fully in chapter 3 on recognising and managing feelings.

There needs to be a balance in our use of questions – too many and a conversation begins to feel like an interrogation. Closed questions (those that can be answered with a yes/no or by repeating a given alternative) have their place as they make less demand on a reticent child. Open, reflective questions, however, encourage a richer response. Here are a few examples:

How do you feel about going into the next class?

What do you think about your new house?

What was it that you found so scary?

Is there anything else you could have said?

How might you do it differently next time?

This kind of questioning holds us back from offering our own solutions to someone else's problem. It invites them instead to explore their own thoughts, feelings and options.

Use of pauses and silence

We are often uncomfortable with pauses in a conversation and so we rush to fill them. In the context of therapeutic conversations pauses are as important as words. We need to recognise just how powerful they can be. They allow the child time to work through an idea, or experience more fully a feeling evoked by the discussion. Pausing also gives a child time to find the words or courage they need to tell a difficult part of their story. Sitting silently rather than responding with a comment or question may be sufficient encouragement for the child to spontaneously expand on what they have already said.

As listeners we need to assess the quality of a silence. We will want to discern whether the child has really finished and handed back to us the turn to talk. Until we get used to using this technique a few seconds' silence will feel much longer to us than it does to the child. As we become more experienced we will find ourselves better able to judge whether some silence is useful or whether the child is discomfited by it. It is a skill we can practise in ordinary conversation and it is interesting to note the effect of leaving some space when the person with whom we are speaking pauses. They may appreciate the opportunity to elaborate on what they were saying.

Barriers to communication

Finally, we need to be aware of some things we may find ourselves doing that get in the way of helping conversations. Unconditional positive regard was mentioned earlier in the chapter. This is also referred to as non-judgemental acceptance. Judging is always counterproductive.

We must be careful not to imply criticism in the way we respond to children, as this simply reinforces their sense of inadequacy or failure and may lead to defensiveness. Our aim instead should be to show understanding of their difficulties.

There are occasions when we may notice ourselves avoiding a child's concerns, which is similarly inadvisable. This is sometimes done by taking the conversation off in a different direction, perhaps because we are uncomfortable with where it is headed. At other times we attempt to apply logic to nullify a child's concerns. Until the child knows that we have genuinely heard those concerns, any attempt to argue against them will undermine their confidence in us. Faulty logic takes time and patience to expose because we have to involve the child in exploration of the available evidence to see that their initial assumption does not hold true. Another way in which concerns are avoided is through premature reassurance. If we try to reassure the child before they are confident we have really heard them, our reassurance will probably be to no avail. The child is more likely to think we are not taking them seriously.

Perhaps the greatest barrier to communication in a helping conversation is the strong temptation to give solutions – the 'if I were you' approach. This presents the adult as expert in the child's difficulties, thereby undermining the child's own insight. We have probably all experienced the frustration of those moments when we simply want to express our feelings, only to find that the one we are talking to just wants to tell us what to do. This is not to say that we cannot make any suggestions. Timing is important, but when the child is ready to engage in problem solving we need to ensure that this is genuinely collaborative. Phrases like 'Some people find it helpful to …' or 'I wonder how it would be if …' can be useful here. We then remain sensitive towards the child's responses, encouraging them to choose the strategy that fits best for them. It is unhelpful to push a child towards a course of action they are uncomfortable with. Rather, we should seek to validate their ideas where possible. We all respond better to encouragement than correction.

Let's get practical

Games

Helping conversations with children can be greatly assisted by introducing a focus activity that provides some structure to the talking. While there are some children who need no encouragement to talk, most find it easier when there is an external activity that reduces the focus on them. There is a large range of therapeutic games, pertinent to different areas of emotional literacy, available through educational suppliers. Children usually relax better during the playing of a game, where the helping adult plays a full part in the turn-taking activities, modelling responses. Many games include question or discussion cards relevant to the topic. Since the time available to play the game will be limited, it is wise to preselect the cards that will be most helpful to address with a specific pupil or group of pupils.

Natural resources

A collection of stones, pebbles, shells, fir cones, acorns, conkers, feathers and twigs is an invaluable creative resource that can be gathered at no cost. The key is to collect items that vary in size, colour, shape and texture. A child can be invited to draw items from the collection to represent themselves and significant people in their lives (family members, peers, teachers). When these are placed on a large sheet of paper or plain cloth, a kind of 'picture' can be developed depicting characteristics and relationships. The helping adult's role is to ask open questions and make reflective comments that gently guide the interaction, e.g. *'I notice that you have put your younger sister right next to Mummy and yourself some distance away. I wonder if that is showing us anything.' 'The stone you have chosen to represent your brother is much bigger than yours. Would you like to say anything about that?' 'Tom's stone has sharp edges and l see lots of sparkly bits in it.' 'The fir cone you have chosen is large and open. How might that be important?'* The adult adopts a stance of interest and curiosity throughout the activity, allowing plenty of time for quiet reflection. Sometimes they may ask questions and sometimes drop in comments that the young person may or may not respond to. A golden rule to observe is never to touch an item the pupil has selected, as in choosing it they have invested it with personal meaning. Touching or moving it would feel intrusive to the child. At the end of the activity, it may be useful to take a photo as a reminder. Always ask children whether they would like to put the objects away themselves or leave them for you to do after they have left.

Miniatures or puppets

A collection of small toys, including cars, figures and other play objects, may be used in the same way as natural objects. Some broken items can usefully be included. The contents of Christmas crackers can be useful additions to the collection. These may be more accessible to younger children because they are less abstract than natural materials. If used with a sandbox, the arrangements become three-dimensional and there is the potential for some things to be part or wholly buried. Engaging with how the child uses the objects is like a journey of discovery for the helping adult. It is not only what they select that is of interest, but how they handle and place them. Stroking an object affectionately and placing it carefully holds different meaning from grabbing it and flinging it carelessly to the edge of the scene.

Finger puppets or larger puppets can be used in a similar way to the miniatures. The adult needs to hold back from prejudging the relevance of their characteristics. To one person a mouse may be thought of as timid, to another as curious and adventurous. Always find out what it means to the child. *'When I asked you to choose something to be you, you quickly chose the mouse. Tell me about the mouse.'*

Drawing

A young person may be invited to draw their fear, for example. They may want to produce a representational picture or an abstract picture. It is important to provide a range of coloured pens, pencils, crayons or pastels for this. While they draw, the adult watches with interest, commenting from time to time on aspects of interest. A child may be invited to draw their family. It is interesting to note who they put where, and sometimes the relative sizes of depicted family members can have a significance beyond their real-life size. A young person who may be the victim of bullying could be invited to draw a sketch map of their school showing safe and unsafe places.

Modelling and craft activities

Clay and playdough are attractive to some pupils because of their kinaesthetic qualities. To mould these may help them relax as they talk. Sometimes there may be relevance to the shapes they create; sometimes it is simply that the activity provides a diversionary focus. There are children who love to engage in craft activities that involve cutting and sticking. It is helpful to have a good range of items such as tissue paper, foil sweet wrappers, pipe cleaners, lolly sticks, paper plates, cups, boxes, and pieces of material. A child may like to make something to show how they feel, something that represents them as a person or a model depicting things that are important in their life.

Case study

Learning about family life

The ELSA was asked to provide a programme of support to Vicky, a 13-year-old girl who was often disruptive in lessons and had received several fixed-term exclusions from school. After meeting several times with Vicky, the ELSA picked up on her dismissive comments about home. Curious to learn more about Vicky's home life, she brought out her collection of natural objects as a focus for a conversation about Vicky's family. Vicky chose a broken pebble to represent herself and put it towards one corner of the large napkin being used for her 'picture'. She acknowledged that it felt like her life had fallen apart when her parents split up. Dad was depicted by a piece of driftwood, flung to the far edge. The ELSA noticed this and commented on how Vicky had cast it to the side. Vicky said her Dad had done that with her – he had walked out and rarely bothered to contact her anymore. She said she didn't care about him anyway, but the ELSA noticed her sad expression and realised Vicky was probably hurting inside. She wondered aloud about how rejecting her father's lack of contact might feel, and Vicky agreed she felt rejected and unimportant. To represent her Mum, Vicky selected a mottled pink pebble which was smooth and rounded. She said her Mum is quite pretty and she used to feel close to her. Then a dishevelled feather was placed alongside. This represented Tom, her Mum's new partner. The ELSA wondered about the feather. *'I don't think he's good enough for Mum. He lounges around drinking beer and watching the telly – never does anything to help. My Mum's always running around after him.'* The ELSA asked how it had felt for Vicky when he moved in. *'I resent him. It's like he's taken my Mum from me,'* Vicky confided. There were several siblings added to the scene, each with their own problems and all of them presenting challenging behaviours at home or in the community. Using the natural objects helped Vicky to describe her frustration with life at home and how she felt unimportant within the family. The ELSA gained a much clearer sense of what it felt like to be Vicky in a family experiencing significant turmoil. Through her empathic understanding, she built good rapport with Vicky and focused her intervention programme on helping her develop a clearer sense of herself – her unique attributes, including her personality traits and special interests, her hopes and fears, and her sense of personal agency (those things she could take control of for herself in life). Vicky's head of year noticed a change in Vicky over the duration of the ELSA intervention. Her marks picked up and her relationship with teachers became less confrontational. Vicky said how much it had helped to be listened to; she felt the ELSA understood and was on her side.

Summary

In this chapter, we have looked at some things we can do to help children feel more comfortable to talk to us. First and foremost is maintaining a positive view of the child regardless of any difficulties they may be presenting. We need to communicate our understanding of where they are at as we listen attentively to the things they choose to share. The importance of non-verbal messages has been considered, both those from the child and those we communicate ourselves. We have included some useful phraseology within therapeutic conversations and noted the importance of leaving space in the conversation for reflection. Some common barriers to successful communication have been noted. A useful expansion of the skills that enhance helping conversations can be found in Gerard Egan's book, *'The Skilled Helper'*. Some practical resources have been suggested as a medium for exploring children's perceptions and experiences.

3. Recognising and managing feelings

Introduction

Emotional literacy can be defined as the ability to recognise, understand, handle and appropriately express your emotions (Sharp 2001). Breaking down this definition emotional literacy encompasses:

- Being aware of the emotions you are experiencing

- Understanding why you might be feeling that way

- Knowing the most effective way for expressing your feelings and being able to put it into action

- Understanding and taking into account the feelings of others, then adjusting your response accordingly.

All of the above can be challenging, even for us as adults, let alone children. We all get it wrong from time to time and we all have ways of responding and dealing with our emotions that are ineffective, often learnt from our parents, those around us or from experience. We learn what works for us in the context of how others react.

The impact of feelings

Feelings have a powerful effect on how we behave. In his book, *'Emotional Intelligence'* (1995), Goleman writes that, 'Emotions that simmer beneath the threshold of awareness can have a powerful impact on how we perceive things and react, even though we have no idea that they are at work.' He describes how the physiology of the brain means that learning and strong emotions compete for space in working memory. Both negative and positive feelings have an influence on learning, memory and problem-solving skills as well as how we relate to others.

Most teachers will have experienced the impact that negative feelings can have in the classroom. Children who come into class feeling angry or upset find it more difficult to concentrate and work to the best of their ability. If they are unable to deal effectively with those uncomfortable feelings, arguments are more likely to occur with their peers or with staff. The result is often a classroom where less learning is taking place and where there is a negative atmosphere. In contrast, children who are able to recognise and effectively manage their feelings are more likely to remember information, learn, problem solve and relate well to other people. Research has found that being able to label your emotions, saying or writing how you are feeling, helps you to regulate your emotions more effectively. In terms of anxiety it has been found that labelling your emotions, saying, "I feel scared" or "I feel anxious" actually reduces the physiological response your body produces in a feared situation (Kircanski, Lieberman and Craske 2012).

Brain physiology

To understand the behaviour of others and ourselves and how our emotions play such an influential role, it is helpful to have a basic understanding of how our brains work. *The MindUp Curriculum* (Hawn Foundation 2011) outlines a simplified model of the three main areas of the brain that play a key role in emotional recognition and regulation; these are the prefrontal cortex, the amygdala and the hippocampus. These three areas try to work together but often get into conflict and struggle against one another.

The amygdala is an emotional processing hub that triggers our fight, flight or freeze response when we feel threatened or stressed in any way. In his book, *'The Chimp Paradox'* (2008), Steve Peters uses the analogy of a chimp to represent this area.

The chimp offers emotional thoughts and feelings that can be destructive or constructive. Peters's book is centred upon finding strategies to help you manage your chimp. The amygdala is the most primitive part of the brain that is present at birth and is critical for survival. It has a powerful impact on our behaviour and gives us the necessary reactions to respond to threat (e.g. running quickly out of the path of oncoming traffic or a sabre-toothed tiger, or as a baby, crying to elicit a response from our carers to meet our need for food or comfort). Many children who have had a difficult start to life and have experienced insensitive, unresponsive caring have learnt that they need to be on high alert all the time. In order to keep themselves safe, their amygdala (the chimp) is easily triggered and they quickly move into fight/flight/ freeze mode. This gets them into all sorts of trouble in the classroom as often they perceive a threat where it does not really exist. Their chimp is in control for much of the time because it is what they have learnt to do in order to survive.

All of us experience times when our chimp hijacks us with thoughts, feelings and behaviour that often we do not want to have. When our amygdala (the chimp) is calm or in a positive emotional state, then incoming information is passed to the prefrontal cortex, the thinking part of the brain. However, when we feel under threat and we are in a negative emotional state, the amygdala prevents the input from being passed to the prefrontal cortex for higher level thinking. The incoming information is left only for the amygdala, the chimp, to process using the automatic fight, flight, freeze responses.

The prefrontal cortex is the area of the brain responsible for learning, reasoning and thinking. This area controls our decision making, helps us to focus our attention and allows us to reason, analyse, predict and plan ahead. Peters talks about this area of the brain being your 'human'. The prefrontal cortex (the human) only gets information when the chimp, the amygdala, is calm. It also passes information on to the hippocampus that is worth remembering.

The hippocampus resides in the temporal lobes. It is the storage area for thoughts and behaviours. It creates, stores and processes all your important facts and memories. Peters likens this area to a computer. It uses the information stored here by the chimp or the human and acts upon it in an automatic way. It controls the types of behaviours where you are on autopilot and do not have to think too hard, because they are well practised behaviours, such as driving or brushing your teeth.

At any one time only one part of the brain is in control in terms of these three key areas.

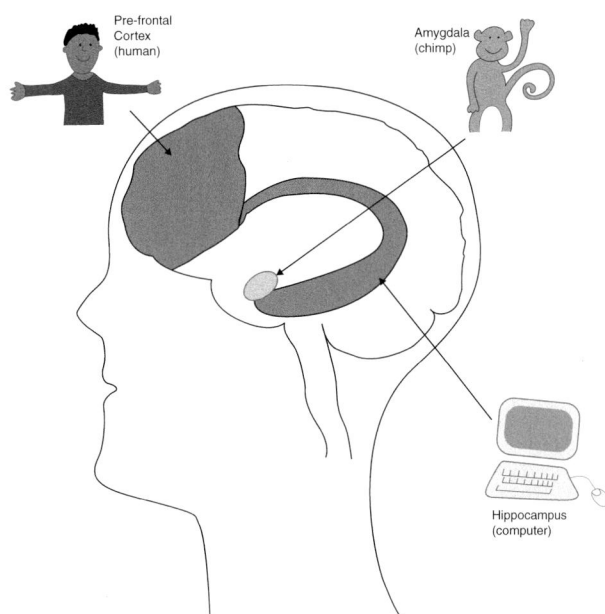

Helping children and young people to have an understanding of which part of their brain is in charge can help them to step back from the situation and put in place strategies that will help them with their emotional regulation.

To start with, this may not happen until after the event has occurred, rather than actually in the situation. For example, John is playing football, which he loves, but he is extremely competitive and has a strong need to win. There is nothing wrong with being competitive, it is just that sometimes, in matches, he ends up being physically violent towards the opposition; his chimp takes over and directs his behaviour. He has a chimp (amygdala) hijack. In the moment, all John's chimp wants is to gain possession of the ball and he has no regard for the rules of fair play or the feelings of his fellow players. His chimp does not think about the future outcomes of its behavior; it just reacts.

To help the prefrontal cortex or 'human' part of the brain take back control, John might use some self-talk, for example, saying to himself, 'Whoa there, I'm getting a bit too angry and excited here, chimp in control, I need to just cool it a bit or I'm going to end up doing something I regret later. Just take a step back, John.' Or it might be that John is not able to take control from his chimp during the situation, but later, with the help of a trusted adult, and if he is familiar with how his brain works, he can talk about which part was in control during an incident.

A helpful tool for successfully managing your emotions, particularly when you are experiencing uncomfortable emotions, such as anger or chronic worry/anxiety, is to recognise that the chimp part of the brain has taken over and that *it* is directing behaviour. The rational, thinking 'human' part of the brain needs to regain control. Even just having this level of awareness about how your brain is working is really helpful for taking a step back and not acting on your feelings. Learning and trying out a range of strategies to help you step back and feel peaceful again, with the prefrontal cortex (the human part of your brain) back in control, is really helpful for successful emotional regulation. Mindfulness/relaxation exercises, self-talk phrases, going for a walk, dancing, taking time to do something different, reading a book, are all examples of strategies people use to help calm their chimp and put the prefrontal cortex (the human) back in the driver's seat. Labelling your emotions when you are experiencing difficult emotions, saying how you are feeling, also helps to diminish those emotions, reducing the amount of activity in the amygdala (Lieberman et al 2007).

Ideas for helping children become more aware of their brain physiology

A useful exercise is outlined in *The MindUp Curriculum*, using hands to represent parts of the brain. Explain to the children that our brains are like the engine inside a car; without it, the car would not move, the lights would not work etc. Ask them to put two fists together with knuckles aligned and thumbs side by side, facing upward. Their brain is about the same size and divided into two halves or hemispheres. The thumbs are the prefrontal cortex – the part that thinks and reasons and plans, the human part. This part of the brain helps you to make good choices and to pay attention.

The tips of their index fingers, buried deep inside – represent the amygdala. The amygdala is the part of the brain we can think of as being like a chimp. It reacts to danger and keeps you safe. It also expresses emotions such as anger, fear and excitement. Although it is good for keeping us safe, sometimes it signals danger when there is none. This then stops the prefontal cortex, the human part of our brain, from thinking and reasoning; the chimp (the amygdala) takes control.

The tips of your middle finger are like the hippocampus. This area is responsible for storing memories, a bit a like a computer.

You can use the diagram shown previously as a visual to illustrate, while you are talking through the function of each part.

Another helpful activity is to put the names of each of the three key brain areas on cards and place them in different areas of the room. Ask the pupil(s) to move to the appropriate card to indicate which part of the brain they think is in control when outlining hypothetical scenarios such as the following:

- Max calls Kieran 'gay boy'. Kieran doesn't react but walks away from Max and thinks to himself, 'It's so not worth it'. (Prefrontal cortex)

- Poppy washes her face, takes off her pyjamas and puts on her school uniform. (Hippocampus)

- Harry has come home from school and goes straight to his bedroom. When he gets there, he realises that someone has been in his room. He shouts downstairs, "How dare you! Who's been messing with my stuff?" (Amygdala)

- A car cuts in front of Charlotte nearly causing an accident. She is tempted to wave her fist and drive too close to him to show her anger. However, she decides to be safe and give the driver the benefit of the doubt. "After all," she reasons, "it's possible he may be on his way to hospital." (Prefrontal cortex)

- Victoria thinks, "I'm just going to go out there and cycle my best and really enjoy it. I'm not going to think that I have to win." (Prefrontal cortex)

- Sam gets in the car and drives his usual route to work. When he gets there he can't remember very much about the journey. (Hippocampus)

- David feels overwhelmed; he says to himself, "I've got to win this tennis match or everyone will be disappointed in me." (Amygdala)

- Jack brushes his teeth before bedtime. (Hippocampus)

- Amelia has a maths test the next day and feels really worried. Thoughts are running through her head. "I'm no good at maths. I can't do it. I'm going to fail." (Amygdala)

- Kelvin is walking down the corridor minding his own business when another boy knocks him on the arm. Kelvin shouts, "Hey!" follows the boy and pushes him from behind. (Amygdala)

- Sally knows where to find her keys as she always leaves them in the same place. (Hippocampus)

Characteristics of pupils who find it difficult to recognise and manage their feelings effectively

- Rarely or never talk about how they are feeling.

- Feeling vocabulary limited to one or two words, e.g. happy, sad.

- Do not ask for help when sad, worried or upset.

- Hurt self, others or property when feeling angry/upset.

- Lack of confidants; do not talk to parents, friends or anyone about their feelings.

- Lack of awareness of how bodily sensations can give them clues to their feelings, e.g., 'I know I am getting angry as my heart starts to beat faster and my palms start to sweat.'

- 'Acting in': quiet, withdrawn, possible self-harm. The message: 'My feelings don't matter, nobody cares about how I feel; nobody wants to know.'

- 'Acting out': aggression towards others and property, verbally abusive. The message: 'This is the only way I know to deal with any uncomfortable feelings I have.'

Activities for developing emotional awareness

The first step in successfully managing emotions is to become more aware of them, recognising how you might be feeling in any particular moment, or being able to identify how you have felt during the day. In addition, being able to recognise what others might be feeling through their facial expression, tone of voice and posture is a key skill to develop.

Younger children

Start with just a few emotions, three or four (or even two depending on the child you are working with). Sad, happy, angry and scared are good emotions to start with. Use a variety of sorting and matching activities to help the child become familiar with facial expressions and postures that signify those emotions.

A few ideas …

- Play snap using '*The Bears*' cards (Veeken 2012). This deck of 48 cards features bear characters showing a wide range of emotions.

- '*A Box Full of Feelings*' (Kog and Moons 2008) is also a very useful resource for this younger age group. It contains four boxes, each with a picture of an emotion on the front. It focuses on four emotions: happy, afraid, angry and sad. You can ask the child/children to post the relevant picture into the appropriate box, e.g., 'He looks happy, so he must go in the box with a happy face on the front.' It also contains finger dolls, masks representing each of the emotions and situational pictures. These pictures show a situation where a child is feeling happy, angry, sad or afraid. The story on the back of the card is then read to the child who has to decide how the person in the picture might be feeling. They can then post them into one of the four boxes.

- Make a mask showing one of the main emotions or draw pictures.

- Play happy and sad music and ask them to move to the music in a happy or sad way.

- Make sad/happy/angry/scared faces in a mirror so they can see how they look or take photographs and display them somewhere with a label.

- Colouring activities: using a sheet of different expressions ask them to colour particular expressions in one colour, e.g. colour all the happy faces yellow and all the sad faces blue.

- Make large posters of the four main emotions to display somewhere prominent.

- Make a book with them using the following titles for each page:

  a) I feel happy when …

  b) I feel sad when …

  c) I feel angry when …

  d) I feel scared when …

- Read a story and talk about the feelings of the characters. Any book for this age range usually has characters experiencing different emotions to talk about. Here are a couple of examples to get you going.

- *'Angry Arthur'* – (Oram 2008) (anger can be a destructive force).
- *'Owl Babies'* – (Waddell 1994) (even baby owls can be scared when mum is late).

Older children (Key Stage 2 and upwards)

- To help pupils become more aware of their feelings it is a good idea to keep a daily record of the most pertinent emotions they have experienced that day. *'The Feelings Diary'* (Shotton 2002) contains photocopiable diary pages so that at some point during the day a pupil can simply circle the pictures that depict the relevant emotions they have experienced. This resource is aimed at KS2 pupils upwards; a simplified version containing fewer emotions would be more suitable for KS1 pupils.

  Often, the most effective way to help pupils develop the daily habit of recording their feelings in the diary is to devote some time in school to the activity. Ten minutes at the end of the day is ideal. Alternatively, a member of staff can spend some time with a pupil where they both complete feelings diaries. This also sends a strong message that taking the time to think about feelings is something that can benefit adults as well as children. What tends to happen if the pupil is given the diary to complete independently is that the good intention of filling it in each day soon wears off. It is a bit like going to the gym; you know it does you good and helps you feel better afterwards, but it is difficult to go when there is something good on the television or more exciting activities are on offer! As well as the photocopiable diary the resource also outlines a six session programme of work which complements the use of the diary. Each session focuses on a different emotion (angry, calm/relaxed, happy, lonely, thankful, and worried); it contains stories, activities, conversation starters and a ten-minute guided relaxation for the session that focuses on feeling calm/relaxed. The sessions are aimed at whole class work but can easily be adapted for one to one or small group work.

- Drawing is a useful activity for exploring and expressing feelings. *'Draw on Your Emotions'* (Sunderland 1993) is a very useful photocopiable manual which aims to help children express and deal more effectively with their emotions through drawing.

- Concentrating on one emotion each week is a useful way to increase pupils' awareness of that emotion and increase emotional awareness generally. In *'Dealing with Feeling'* Tina Rae outlines 20 sessions each focusing on a different feeling. The resource is aimed at whole class or small groups but the stories, questions and many of the activities would also be very useful on a one to one basis.

The emotional literacy traffic lights approach

Stepping back from a situation, rather than jumping in impulsively when we have a chimp hijack and feel angry or upset, is a difficult skill to acquire. We can all recall situations where we have simply 'gone with the flow' of our emotions and regretted our words or actions later. For many pupils this lack of self-control impacts significantly on their behaviour in school and is a common reason for pupils becoming excluded. In his book '*Emotional Intelligence*' (1995), Daniel Goleman describes a traffic lights approach for helping to teach impulse control to pupils. Tina Rae has adapted this approach in her book, '*Dealing with Feeling*', mentioned above. The idea is that pupils become familiar with the traffic light stages. Red indicates the need to stop rather than just react. We need to resist the urge to react in a nasty or aggressive way even if we feel like doing so. Amber indicates that next we need to wait, to give ourselves time to develop a more effective action plan. We need to look at our options and reflect on plans we might have made beforehand about what we might do or say in such a situation. It should be noted that sometimes we need to stay on amber for quite a long time, longer than traffic lights do. The amber phase may need to last for 20 minutes or an hour or a day. Green indicates that now it is time to put our plan into action.

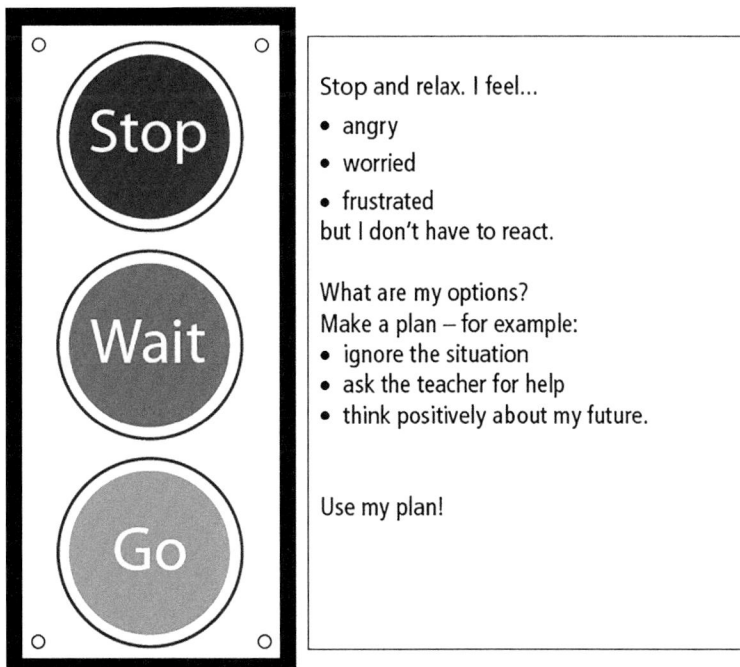

Stop and relax. I feel...
- angry
- worried
- frustrated
but I don't have to react.

What are my options?
Make a plan – for example:
- ignore the situation
- ask the teacher for help
- think positively about my future.

Use my plan!

Case study

Putting the traffic light approach into action, a case study

Jack, a year ten pupil, found that his impulsive reactions to situations would often get him into trouble. He would feel overwhelmed with feelings of anger and frustration and react aggressively towards his peers or towards school staff. He often shouted at the teacher, banged the desk, lashed out physically at others and then stormed out. Later he regretted his actions and was genuinely remorseful, but that did not seem to stop him subsequently repeating his behaviour on another occasion. The traffic light approach was introduced to Jack. Together we created some useful phrases that he could say to himself at each stage. These were written on a card displaying the traffic light sequence. Jack kept the card in his pocket just as a reminder to use when he needed it. We talked through a number of situations that were pertinent triggers for his anger and thought through the options that were available to him in those situations. A particularly powerful trigger was two girls who would often make derogatory comments towards him in humanities lessons. Jack's solution for dealing with this difficult situation was simply to ignore the girls. In order to do this, I knew he would need something specific he could focus on, as ignoring is a very difficult thing to do when you feel threatened. Jack was keen to go to college when he finished school, but he knew he would not be able to unless he performed well in his exams, and that meant staying in lessons. He decided that to visualise himself at college would help him to maintain his self-control in the situation. He knew that a lack of self-control would jeopardise his future.

Jack met with his head of year each week to review his plan and tweak it if necessary. He found that he did not need the card after a couple of weeks as he could then simply remember the sequence. Keeping the traffic light sequence in mind really helped him to stop and think things through before reacting.

Summary

Emotional literacy is the ability to recognise, understand and appropriately express your emotions. It's fair to say that all of us struggle at times to recognise what we might be feeling, express our feelings effectively and also recognise the feelings of others. A first step in developing emotional literacy skills is to start to recognise your feelings and work out ways you can manage those emotions that will work for you. A range of practical ideas and resources for developing the ability to read and express emotions effectively are outlined in this chapter. Additionally, the chapter contains ideas for gaining more insight into the physiology of your brain and how the different parts are integral to how we process and manage our emotions.

4. Self-esteem

Introduction

How we see and evaluate ourselves has a significant impact on our thinking and subsequent behaviour. Street and Isaacs (1998) distinguish self-esteem as being different from self-perception, describing it as an individual's evaluative assessment of their self-perception. We all have an idea of how we think we should be, our ideal self; self-esteem can be thought of as how well we think we measure up to how we think we should be. In her book, '*Self–Esteem: A Family Affair*' (1998), Jean Illsley Clarke describes self-esteem as believing that you are capable as well as lovable. Fundamental to self-esteem is having an unconditional acceptance of oneself. If we accept ourselves as we are, appreciating all that is positive and unique about ourselves as well as accepting our negative characteristics, then we are more likely to have a positive view of ourselves. In his hierarchy of human needs, Maslow includes self-esteem as being a fundamental need that we all have. He identifies two separate self-esteem needs, the need for the respect and admiration of others and the need for positive self-regard.

Those working in schools and children's homes come across many children and young people who have a very negative view of themselves. They do not like who they are and see themselves as being unlovable and unacceptable. Low self-esteem may manifest itself in many ways: some children may become quiet and withdrawn, others may feel the need to prove themselves and come across as being loud and possibly disruptive, and others may become perfectionists in order to gain the approval and acceptance of people around them.

How do we end up seeing and evaluating ourselves in the way that we do? Where does our self-perception and consequently our self-esteem come from?

Michele Borba (1989) identifies five building blocks of self-esteem:

1. Security
2. Selfhood
3. Affiliation
4. Mission
5. Competence.

In this chapter we will be taking each of these building blocks and explore in turn what it is, the psychological theories which link in to it and practical ideas for developing each aspect with children and young people.

1. Security (trusting, warm relationships)

The importance of the sensitivity and quality of care, particularly in the first three years of life, is now well established. It was Bowlby (1953) who first outlined the importance of having a secure attachment to a primary caregiver. Over the past 20 years, with developments in neuro-scanning technology, we can now see the positive impact of a child having a secure, trusting relationship with their caregiver. In this type of relationship, the caregiver is sensitive to the needs of the child and creates a relationship where the child learns they can trust the adult. This results in the development of neural pathways and brain growth. We can also see the direct result of the lack of a secure relationship which impacts negatively on brain development (Teicher and Sanson 2016).

With high quality and sensitive care, children *'come to expect a world that is responsive to their feelings and helps to bring intense states back to a comfortable level; through the experience of having it done for them, they learn to do it themselves'* (Gerhardt 2004). The importance of security is also summed up very well in the following quote from Howe (2005), *'The more secure children feel, the more time, energy and inclination they have to seek understanding and make sense. Whereas fear constricts, safety expands the range of exploration.'*

It is through these primary relationships that the child comes to develop what Bowlby called their 'internal working model'. This is how they see themselves, others and the world. The quality of care and attunement will impact on how lovable and acceptable a child comes to see themselves as being. All the time through relationships, messages are being sent to them about how worthy they are of attention and care, that they are worth spending time with, that what they do is interesting. Alternatively, a child may receive messages through neglect and rejection that they are not lovable and acceptable. Children who have experienced neglect or abuse often come to believe that adults are not to be relied on and that they need to try to meet their own needs. Children who lack this sense of security, who have not had, and do not currently have, a secure trusting relationship, frequently do not feel safe and rarely relax; it is much harder for them to explore and learn.

How can we develop a secure trusting relationship with the children in school even if they have not experienced this at home? This can be difficult but with perseverance it is possible.

In their book, *'The 5 Love Languages of Children'*, Chapman and Campbell (2012) describe the helpfulness of identifying a child's preferred love language – physical touch, words of affirmation, quality time, gifts or acts of service. While these may all be appreciated, a child will have a primary love language preference. When their need in this area is not met, they may feel unloved. If quality time is what they crave, the giving of gifts will be an inadequate way for a parent to communicate their love. Once the preferred love language is understood and the child receives quality time, for example, their sense of being loved increases and their behaviour improves. Even if this need is not being met within the family, a key adult in school may recognise that a child who always seeks adult company at playtime, for example, may be expressing a need for quality time. Building in special time with an adult in school will at least meet the child's need in that context. If the primary need is physical touch, then appropriate contact such as a pat on the back, gentle touching of the arm or tousling of a younger child's hair can be a very powerful communication of appreciation. Words of affirmation note a child's personal qualities, effort and achievements. Acts of service involve offering help in areas meaningful to the child. Gifts may seem problematic, but these can be very simple things like a picture from a magazine of the child's favourite footballer.

Practical ideas for developing security:

- Listening to the child and trying to understand how they see things in their world.

- Taking an interest in the things that interest them.

- Spending time sharing a fun activity with the child.

- Seeking opportunities that show the child you care and that they matter to you.

- Being consistent in behaviour and expectations, keeping the boundaries clear.

- Dan Hughes talks about using PACE. PACE stands for an attitude that is Playful, Accepting, Curious and Empathic. He has found that when adults use a playful approach, sharing humour with the child, when they express curiosity rather than judgement about the child's behaviour, when they are accepting of the child as they are and when they demonstrate empathy towards the child, this helps to build a trusting relationship, even with children who have experienced abuse or neglect in the past. They are more likely to relax and can settle to learn (Bomber and Hughes 2013).

2. Selfhood

Borba describes this aspect of self-esteem as being a feeling of individuality and uniqueness. The child has an accurate, realistic and positive view about themselves in terms of their physical characteristics, personality and attitudes. One of the indicators of a good sense of selfhood that Borba outlines is that the child is comfortable accepting praise. Conversely, children who have a weak sense of selfhood might frequently use negative statements to describe themselves, be uncomfortable with how they look and find it hard or be unable to say anything positive about themselves.

Practical ideas for developing a sense of selfhood

With younger children, help them to develop a more accurate self-description through drawing round themselves on a large sheet of paper and writing about their physical and personality characteristics inside the outline.

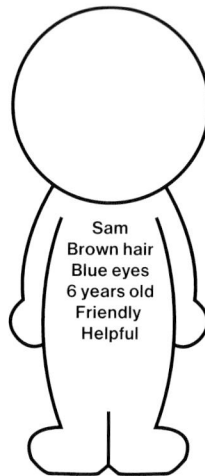

For older children, making a wanted poster can help in developing a sense of selfhood. Here they draw a picture of themselves, or a photo can be used, and underneath they describe their characteristics.

3. Affiliation/belonging

Borba describes this building block as being a feeling of belonging, acceptance, or relatedness, particularly in relationships that are considered important; feeling approved of, appreciated, and respected by others. In Maslow's hierarchy, he identifies the need to belong as being a fundamental need we all have and essential for achieving a sense of self-worth and eventually self-actualisation. If children and young people do not feel they belong, particularly in the school years, they will strive to be accepted by a group. There are exceptions of course and the need to belong is stronger in some individuals than in others. Groups have a significant impact on our behaviour and this can be positive as well as negative depending on the group subculture. The need to belong is so strong that it can override the values and beliefs a young person has been brought up with and accepted all their lives.

If we do not feel that we belong to any group, family or friends, this can have an impact on our mental health. A study by Hagerty and Williams (1999) found that feeling as though you do not belong was a predictor of depression. School can be a very lonely place when you feel you do not have any friends, or that you do not belong. School staff can help tremendously by doing some subtle social engineering to help a young person develop positive friendships. Children may need input on the skills of friendship, how to make and keep friends, as well as help in establishing a social group.

Practical ideas for developing affiliation

- Set up a circle of friends around the young person (for further details see chapter 6 on friendship skills).

- Team the young person up for jobs and tasks with one or two peers with whom you think they can form a relationship.

- For times when a lack of belonging may be more apparent, e.g. break times, it may be helpful to give the young person a job to do on the playground, e.g. organising a playground game or being a playground buddy.

- Look at possible extra-curricular clubs the child might be interested in, both at school and beyond.

- Encourage parents/carers to invite other children for social events outside school hours; having a friend round to play at your house creates a whole new dimension to the relationship.

4. Mission

Borba defines this as having a feeling of purpose and motivation in life. You have a sense of self-empowerment through setting realistic and achievable goals and being willing to take responsibility for the consequences of your decisions. A young person who lacks mission may feel powerless and appear aimless. Their goals are either too high, too low or non-existent and they may have a tendency to avoid taking responsibility for their actions.

Self-determination theory was created by Deci and Ryan (2009). It is a theory of motivation that looks at why people make the choices they do and what will sustain them on their path. They outline that we have three basic needs which, when met, lead us to the highest quality of motivation and wellbeing. One of our key needs is 'autonomy'. This is the need we have to feel 'choiceful' as though we have made an active decision to pursue something. If we feel we have chosen to do something our motivation is more likely to be high. The ideas around mission fit well with Deci and Ryan's concept of autonomy.

In many ways the ideas around mission also share strong links with developing a growth mindset. Carol Dweck (2012) found that we all have varying beliefs about the underlying nature of our abilities. People with a growth mindset believe that intelligence and abilities can be developed through effort and persistence, through trying different strategies and learning from your mistakes. People with a fixed mindset believe that intelligence and abilities are static, something that you are born with and that you don't have the power to change. With a fixed mindset, failure means that you are just not good enough and cannot get better. When people feel this way, they get disheartened and give up. People with a growth mindset, however, believe that they can get better at things through practice, so when faced with a challenge they become more determined to succeed. Researchers have found that building a growth mindset helps children become more motivated and engaged in activities; they are more likely to make progress and try new things.

Practical ideas for developing a sense of mission

- Giving them an element of choice in a task. It promotes autonomy and helps them to develop intrinsic motivation for a task if they feel they have actively chosen something rather than a task being forced upon them.

- Helping them in setting realistic goals. Asking them what they want to achieve and taking the time to discuss their aspirations and goals with them.

- Providing opportunities for them to check on their progress.

- Allowing them to discover the consequences of their actions.

- It is important to communicate the message that change is always possible and that, with time and effort, we can all improve our skills. The brain is always growing and changing; we can train our brains to learn new things!

- Praise the effort rather than internal attributes; so rather than telling a pupil that they did something because they are clever, or even, as is so often heard in school, 'clever boy/girl', try to use alternative phrases such as:

- You tried hard really hard with that

- I'm impressed that you didn't give up, you kept going, even when you were finding it hard

- You have really improved your ... skills

- You really handled that situation well because ...

- You remembered to bring ... to school

- You must have taken some time at home to learn ....

Encourage them to use positive self-talk:

Instead of	Try saying to yourself
I'm no good at this, I can't do this	What am I missing?
I give up	I'll try using some of the strategies I've learnt
I can't do maths	I'm going to train my brain in maths
I always make so many mistakes	Mistakes help me to learn better
This is too hard	This may take some time and effort

5. Competence

This aspect of self-esteem also links well with self-determination theory mentioned earlier (Deci and Ryan 2009). As well as the need for autonomy, another fundamental need that Deci and Ryan identify for maximum wellbeing and motivation is that of competence. Competence is described as feeling effective in things the person regards as being important or valuable. They are aware of their strengths and willing to accept their weaknesses. We are attracted to activities in which we feel competent so that this need will be satisfied.

Practical ideas for developing a sense of competence

- Encourage the child to try a number of different clubs and activities to explore what they might like and what they feel good at.

- When introducing a new activity, e.g. learning to play the recorder, try to ensure the child is not going to be in a group where they feel a sense of incompetence because the others are already far ahead of them. This is a sure way to put them off a new activity.

- Charting competencies, finding hidden treasure!

  This is a powerful technique that Ioan Rees (2005) describes as part of a solution orientated approach. You have a conversation with the pupil, getting them to talk about their hobbies, interests, holidays etc. in order to discover skills (what they can do), strengths (what they are good at) and resources (those who know the person has these skills).

A few suggested phrases ...

> I'd really like to take the chance to get to know you more so I'd like to hear about the sorts of things that you enjoy doing, or think you might be good at.

> What could you start by telling me? What would you say you are quite good at? It can be at home or at school.

As they talk about the things they like doing (e.g. playing on the PlayStation, cycling etc.) you draw more out of them about it. How often they do it, where and when, what they have achieved with it etc. You need to listen really closely because you are looking for hidden treasure, what those activities tell you about the strengths a youngster may possess that are unique to him/her.

> So, playing on the PlayStation for four hours. I couldn't do that, I think I'd lose concentration. What does that tell us about you? (Hopefully the young person will be able to identify their ability to concentrate for long periods but if not, prompt them.) What do you have to do to get high scores in the game? So, you have to co-ordinate which buttons you press with what you see on the screen. Is it OK if you do that slowly or do you have to be quick? (Try to draw out that they must have good reflexes as well as good hand-eye co-ordination.) And you just keep going with it? You see, I'd get fed up and give up but you don't, you just keep going. Do you know what that's called? That's called perseverance, the ability to keep going. That's great; I'm going to write that down here, 'perseverance'.

Then you find out about who else knows of this skill/strength.

> Who else apart from me knows you're so good at playing on the PlayStation?

> If they were here right now, what else would they tell me about you that would be interesting?

As the conversation goes on, the responses can be recorded on a chart like the one that follows. Of course, you do not have to write down the answers on a chart.

Activity	Skill	Strength	Who knows about this
Playing on Play Station	Good reflexes Hand eye co-ordination	Concentration Perseverance	Mum
Cycling	Good balance Fitness	Gets back on bike when falls off – courage	Granddad

At the end of the session, take the time to feed back to the pupil all that you have learned about him/her, outlining to them the strengths that have been revealed.

- Use strength cards (cards that outline a number of strengths a young person may have). These can be bought commercially, or you can make your own. The advantage of making your own is that you can gear them to the age of the children you are working with and the sorts of images that they relate to. Here are a few examples.

Good at sharing

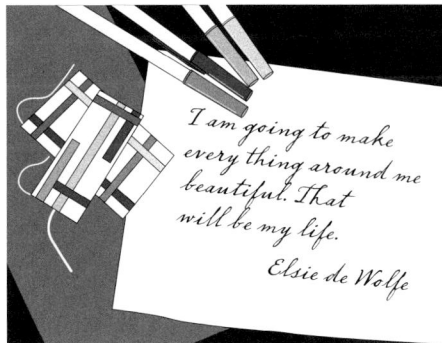

Lovely writing

Good memory

53

Good at singing

- Working with an individual you can get the young person to sort the cards into three piles, those that are definitely like them, sometimes like them and not like them at all.

- In a whole class circle time activity, you can spread out all the cards in the middle of the circle and each person has to select a card for the person on their right and say why they chose it.

- Tree of life.

A good follow-up activity to using the strength cards is to show the children how to draw a tree to represent different parts of their lives. This activity is taken from narrative psychology practice and supports all the building blocks of self-esteem which Borba identifies.

In the trunk the children write about their skills and abilities, where they feel a sense of competence. In the ground they write and draw about some of the activities they currently enjoy in and out of school. The roots represent where they come from, their family history and

extended family, people who have had an influence on them and taught them things in their lives. They use the branches to outline their hopes and dreams for the future, the direction they want their lives to go in. On the leaves they identify the people in their life that they value and hold as precious. Finally, they draw a piece of fruit beside each person they identify on the leaves, and on each fruit they state what they have received from that person, e.g. being cared for or encouraged by them.

The tree of life activity can facilitate numerous conversations that are very helpful for building self-esteem. You can do it on an individual basis or in a group/whole class. If doing it as a group/whole class activity it allows you to ask the children to identify strengths that they see in their peers and they can then write these on the others' trees using small post-it notes. It's a great way to build a positive classroom climate where the children get to know and appreciate one another more, as well as getting to know themselves better.

Summary

Self-esteem is the degree to which you believe you are lovable and capable. Parents, teachers and friends all have an important impact on self-esteem as a child develops. Low self-esteem may manifest itself in many ways. Some children may become quiet and withdrawn; others may feel the need to prove themselves and come across as being loud and possibly disruptive; yet others may become perfectionists in order to gain the approval and acceptance of those around them. Borba outlines five key building blocks of self-esteem. Practical ideas for working with a pupil (or pupils) to help improve their self-esteem are contained within this chapter.

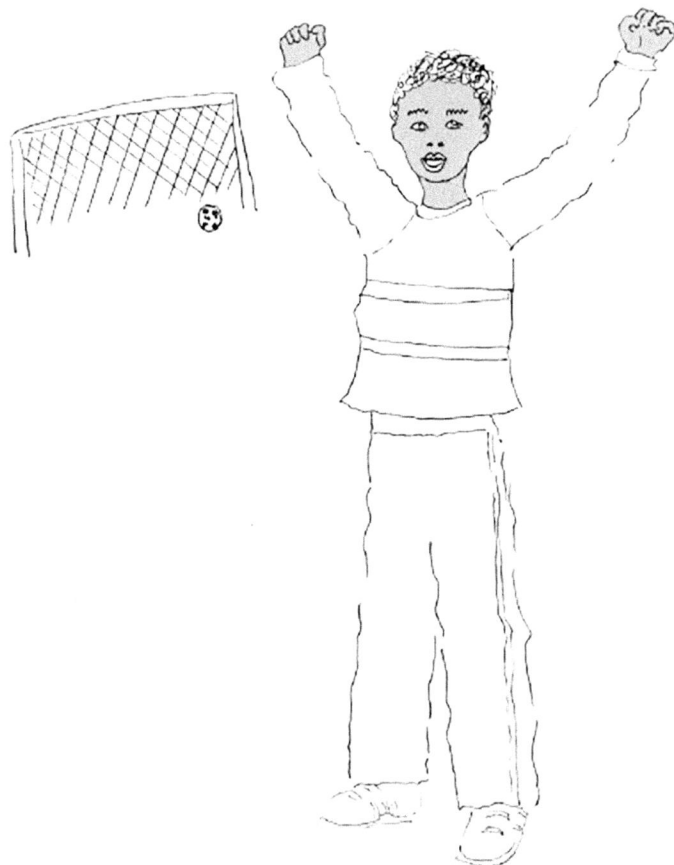

5. Working with uncomfortable emotions

Introduction

In chapter 3, *Recognising and managing feelings*, we discussed the impact of different areas of the brain upon behaviour. Emotional regulation requires effective integration of emotional responses and cognitive reasoning. This is relevant to the full range of feelings, those we seek more of as well as those we would prefer to reduce. Uncontrolled excitement creates risks for us, just as uncontrolled anger or anxiety does. If we fail to regulate our excitement we may make impulsive responses that we later regret. In this chapter, we look at learning to regulate uncomfortable emotions like anger and anxiety which, if they overwhelm us, can have a negative impact on our social relationships and the achievement of our life goals.

Psychologist Jonathan Haidt (2006) used the metaphor of an elephant and its rider to describe two sides of human nature – an emotional/automatic/irrational side (the elephant) and an analytical/controlled/rational side (its rider). This model suggests the elephant is irrational, driven by emotion and instinct, while the rider is rational and can plan a course of action. The challenge is to balance the two sides. The elephant can take over at times (when automatic and emotional responses prevail) and the rider can pull the elephant back on track (by thinking through emotional meaning and the consequences of actions).

We start from the premise that all emotions have value and are an essential expression of our humanity. Unfortunately, our emotional responses are not always accurate or helpful. Thoughts, imagination and misinterpretations can lead to unnecessary or unhelpful reactions. We may react to a threat that is either absent or unlikely, such as feeling anxious on a flight in case the plane crashes. We may displace unresolved frustration at school or at work by taking it out on a parent or partner at home. Emotional literacy is about learning to work productively with our emotions by questioning, understanding and regulating them. It is known that emotional health has a direct impact on physical health. Excessive stress and high levels of anxiety are known to contribute to heart disease, for example. Positive emotional experiences are known to release endorphins, natural chemicals in the brain that decrease pain and feelings of stress and enhance the immune system. Through psycho-education, we can learn how to use our rational mind to regulate our emotional responses.

The cognitive-behavioural model

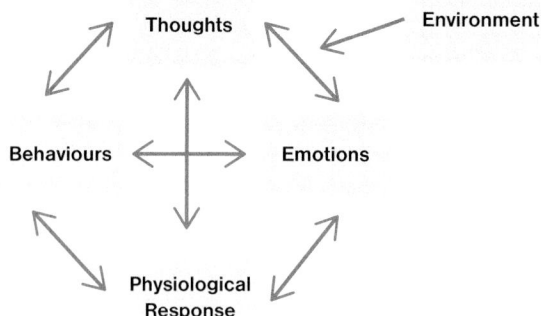

This model comes from cognitive behaviour therapy (CBT) and combines basic principles from behavioural and cognitive psychology. CBT is based on the belief that distorted thinking and maladaptive behaviours lead to psychological disorders such as anxiety and depression. The diagram above describes the interaction between thoughts, emotions, physiological responses and behaviours that occur in response to the things we encounter in our environment. The thoughts include the things we say to ourselves, images and memories. Physiological responses refer to bodily reactions such as changes in heart rate, muscle tension, perspiration and physical tiredness. Behaviour includes the things we say and do in response to these. Each of these elements interacts with each of the others. Hence our thoughts feed our emotions, but our emotions also influence our thoughts. All four elements interact, not necessarily in equal amounts, at any one time. The emphasis in this model is how, by realigning our thinking, we can modify our emotional and physiological states and our consequent behaviour. For example, we hear a loud knock on the door. If the immediate thought is, 'It's probably a delivery,' the reaction will be different from our response to the automatic thought, 'Someone's bringing bad news.' In the former case, we may be startled by the knock but remain calm as we go to the door, whereas in the latter case, panic begins to set in.

When working with children in school whose thinking has become distorted by negative expectation, it is possible, with the aid of good resources, to use some of the principles from CBT without undergoing training as a cognitive behavioural therapist. An excellent resource is Paul Stallard's book, '*Think Good – Feel Good*' (2003). This is a workbook that presents the key principles of CBT in an accessible way for children, incorporating attractively designed worksheets.

To work with a child using this model, it will be necessary to check the child's understanding of their emotions (recognising and naming them), their awareness of physiological changes that accompany them and how well they can articulate their thoughts. Identifying areas of difficulty enables the setting of targets for intervention. Useful resources include emotions pictures (available in many forms, but one of our favourites being the Bear Cards), a body outline for illustrating physiological responses and published resources such as *The Big Book of Blob Trees* by Pip Wilson and Ian Long (2009). The Blobs are ageless and genderless human representations drawn to express many life scenarios with which people may identify. Working with them can help draw out children's thoughts and experiences.

Understanding and managing anger

Anger can be one of the strongest and most destructive emotions that we experience. In its most extreme form it leads one human being to take the life of another. Whole societies are ripped apart as one group seeks the destruction of a rival group. It destroys families and friendships. Directed towards the self it saps the will to live, driving some to extreme forms of self-harm and even suicide.

But is it all negative? Should we aspire to live without any expression of anger? On the contrary, since anger is an essential characteristic of our humanity, we need to recognise its value and purpose in our lives. Anger on a societal level has led to struggles against injustice, like young children being forced prematurely into a life of hard labour down coal mines or up chimneys. William Wilberforce battled most of his life for the abolition of slavery. His tireless efforts led to sustained social reform within British society. Anger can provide motivation to work towards important change on a personal level as well, like extricating oneself from an abusive relationship. As a response to threat, anger gives rise to the protection of self and others from perceived dangers.

The challenge lies in managing such a powerful emotion so that the resulting behaviours remain under our reasoned control, ensuring as far as possible the safety of both ourselves and those around us. Like any other behaviour, anger ultimately is a choice. We choose when and how to give it expression. The choices we make are strongly influenced by our life experiences, not least by the role models around us. We often stick stubbornly to learned behaviours, even when they are less effective than we wish in achieving the ends we desire. But if most behaviour is learned, then it follows that it may also be unlearned. For children and young people in school, the support of an understanding and supportive adult may be crucial – one who will take the time to help them understand uncomfortable feelings and encourage them to make safer choices.

The assault cycle

This was developed in 1997 by Glynis Breakwell to support those coping with the aggressive behaviour of others. Older children sometimes find it helpful to have this explained to them to help them understand the stages they go through in an angry outburst and what happens in their bodies. The trigger phase is where an angry response is sparked; this is the best point at which to defuse it by diverting attention to something else or by using calming strategies. At this point chemicals are being released in the brain and bloodstream that increase alertness and provide a burst of energy. They are preparing the body for the fight-or-flight response and it is these chemicals that produce the physiological changes described in a later section. They are released rapidly, leading to speedy escalation of anger and are accompanied by an increased potential for aggression. Unless there is quick action to calm the situation, the crisis phase is reached, which represents the height of the outburst. At this point emotionality supersedes rationality. It takes much longer for the chemicals to dissipate than it took for them to be released initially. The angry child is susceptible during this recovery phase to the triggering of further aggressive responses, so this is not the time to discuss the incident or issue punishments. Whereas recovery can be rapid in very small children, the duration of the recovery phase increases significantly in adolescence. In the post-crisis depression stage, the child or young person often feels guilty and negative about themselves. At this stage, they need reassurance that all is not lost. Only when their arousal has returned to baseline level is it appropriate to begin talking about what has happened, any consequences resulting from the angry behaviour and to discuss possible alternative responses for the future.

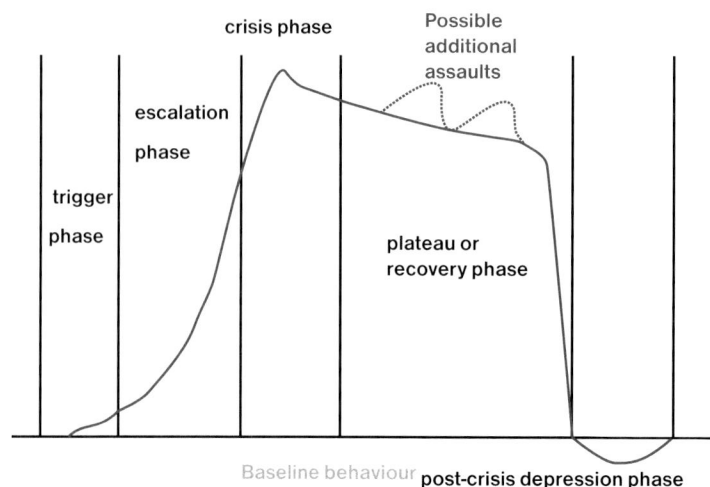

The assault cycle – Breakwell 1997

Let's get practical

The sections below present a good structure for working through an anger management programme with children, either individually or in a group.

Normalising anger

When working with youngsters who have difficulty handling frustration and give vent to frequent outbursts of anger, it is important first to acknowledge the legitimacy of angry feelings. It is unhelpful for them to be left thinking that anger is an unacceptable emotion that needs to be repressed and denied. Anger which is persistently turned in may lead to depression. This is not to suggest that it is healthy to be frequently angry, but it is appropriate to acknowledge that anger is a normal part of human experience. This is shown by the wide range of vocabulary in our language that denotes degrees of anger – cross, annoyed, irritated, frustrated, stressed, upset, mad, furious and enraged. The more adept we become at articulating our feelings, the less dependent we will be on acting them out in more overt ways.

A good starting place then is work around the vocabulary associated with anger. This need not be restricted to words meaning anger, but could encompass physical signs like changes in heart rate, breathing and colour (becoming pale or reddening of the face), increased muscle tension and perspiration, increased fidgeting and churning stomach. Behavioural signs of anger can also be explored, like hitting, punching, kicking, shouting, swearing and crying. In this way pupils can be helped to appreciate that everyone feels angry sometimes, and that we can show it in different ways. Brainstorming as many words associated with anger as possible is a safe and non-threatening way to begin work around anger, perhaps representing some of them through drawings. A collection could be made of pictures cut from magazines or downloaded from the internet. Clip art is a rich source of illustrations.

The firework model

A useful model for thinking about anger is the firework model, as described by Faupel, Herrick and Sharp (1998).

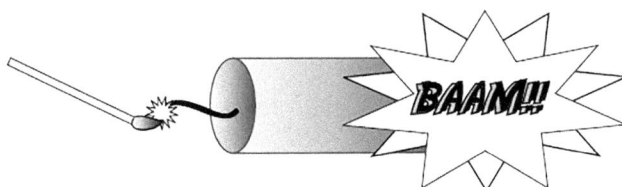

The trigger is represented by a match that lights our fuse. The fuse represents our mind reacting through thoughts and emotions. If the fuse burns unchecked the firework, representing physiological reactions, eventually explodes. The explosion represents the behavioural expression of the physiological tensions that build up inside us. It may be small and unimpressive like an indoor firework, or it may be like the spectacular explosion of a large rocket, sparks flying in all directions.

This has proved a useful model in helping even very young children understand what happens when we become angry. It provides a way of talking about angry outbursts, enabling reflection on what gave rise to the angry feelings in the first place (the trigger), how the trigger was being interpreted by the child (the fuse) and the resulting behaviour (the exploding firework). In thinking about anger in this way, it can be helpful and more engaging for the child if discussion is accompanied by actually making the model.

The firework model also provides a natural sequence for working with a pupil on safe ways of managing angry feelings. There is always a temptation for adults to want to leap straight in and suggest defusing strategies without first doing the all-important groundwork. It is the preparatory groundwork that helps to develop the trusting relationship between adult and young person. Without this, there may be a tacit defensiveness and resistance to change.

The trigger

Adult and young person can think together about things that lead them to feel angry. They are likely to discover that, while they have some triggers in common, certain things that induce strong, angry feelings in one of them may be quite a neutral experience for the other. This could be done as a brainstorm but may be easier if a list of potential triggers is supplied. A rating scale against each item on the list would allow comparison of the relative strength of the various triggers, although it is also useful to reflect on the way our responses vary according to how we are feeling at the time. When we are relaxed and happy we can usually tolerate greater frustration than when we are tired or unwell.

The fuse

This is the part of the model that links closely with cognitive behavioural approaches, discussed earlier in the chapter. At this point the emphasis turns to how our interpretation of events influences our feelings. An extremely powerful way of illustrating this is to present a series of visual illusion pictures. These help to make the point that two people can look at the same picture and see quite different things. This is not only true of pictures, but also of situations and events. Situational pictures could then be used to reinforce this, with each person suggesting a different story behind the picture. Work around personal perception is very important, since the way we think about things can intensify or neutralise our feelings about them.

This prepares the way for work on cognitive reframing – choosing to adopt an alternative perspective. When angry feelings are triggered we can power them up by choosing to dwell on negative thoughts that feed anger and depression (e.g. 'She really hates me'), or we can find ways of talking ourselves up (e.g. 'She's a bit stressed today – she's usually more patient than that'). Angry and depressing thoughts tend to over-personalise the other person's negative response, whereas reframed thinking pays greater attention to the context in which the response occurred. Helping a young person recognise their tendency to over-personalise and change the way they think is likely to take considerable practice and patience, as thought patterns can be deeply engrained.

Physiological changes

It is useful to help pupils become aware of the physical symptoms that accompany their mounting anger, things like:

- Getting fidgety
- Becoming hot and sweaty
- Racing heart beat
- Breathing more quickly
- Tensing muscles
- Churning stomach.

These can then become early warning signals to a pupil that they need to start choosing how they will manage their angry feelings.

One way of helping a pupil who has not noticed any physical signs is to ask them to remember a time when they felt really angry. Ask them to try to picture themselves back in that situation, remembering who was there and what was happening. Encourage them to feel the anger again and to start drawing it. They could draw what happened or make an abstract representation of their feelings. As they do this, ask them to notice what is happening in their body. You may need to suggest some of the possible changes so that they understand what to look for, and you may notice, for them, some changes in their demeanour. Help them to make a list of all the physical signs that they experience. This could be done on an outline sketch of the body.

They could begin to keep a log of times they feel angry, noting the trigger, noting the thoughts and physical feelings they had, and noting what happened (whether they exploded or found a way to calm down). You could create a blank log book for them with three boxes for each event, marked 'trigger', 'fuse' and 'actions'. Pupils with less developed literacy skills would need the support of a teacher, classroom assistant or parent to fill it in once they had recovered from the incident.

Calming strategies

The foundation has now been laid for exploring ways of keeping angry feelings under control. Sometimes adults make the mistake of telling children what they ought to do, rather than taking time to explore strategies which the pupil believes might work for them. It should not be assumed that an angry pupil has never used any calming strategies. Rather, it is worth asking if they can think of a time when they felt angry but managed not to lose their temper, or not to lose it very badly. If they can, explore with them what they were doing at that time. This is known as looking for exceptions. If a strategy has been used successfully in the past, the pupil may be encouraged to use it again. It may also give a clue to other calming strategies that might suit them.

Some possible calming strategies are:

- Sit down. Close your eyes. Relax. Take a deep breath in then let it out very slowly. Repeat this several times.

- Clench all the muscles in your body, starting at your head and working down to your toes. Then work down your body and relax them again, letting all the tension drain away.

- Turtle technique – imagine you have a protective shell to withdraw into, and shut yourself off from the situation.

- Take your mind somewhere else that feels safe, e.g. imagine yourself curled up in bed, or in another favourite place having fun. Try to imagine the sights, sounds, smells and textures.

- Count slowly to ten, or to 100! Try counting backwards, or counting in threes. If your mind is occupied with something else, it cannot dwell on the problem.

- Keep repeating a short phrase to yourself (in your mind or under your breath) like 'Cool it!' or 'I can get over this'.

- Remove yourself from the situation that is annoying you. This gives you space to think of something else.

- Do some physical activity – running, playing ball, punching the air or a pillow. Physical exercise gets rid of some of the chemicals that build up in your body when you are angry.

- Listen to some favourite music – something restful or something that makes you happy.

- Remember something funny – a favourite joke or comedy scene. It is difficult to laugh and be angry at the same time!

In reality, we need a range of calming strategies to suit different situations. Some will be more suitable for home or out in the playground, and others can be helpful within the confines of a classroom. It is important to help pupils select appropriate strategies for the different places where they sometimes lose their temper. Sometimes they are helped by a prompt card that they keep in their pocket. There are a range of published games that help pupils think of ways of staying calm.

Expressing angry feelings effectively

Anger management is not simply about suppressing angry feelings though. Sometimes it is important to let people know that things they are doing are causing us a problem. This is best done when we are calm otherwise we tend to say things we later regret. It also helps if we remain respectful towards the other person, avoid a blaming tone and tell them factually about the difficulty. It is helpful to name the behaviour that has upset us, the effect it has on us and offer a preferred solution.

Here are a few examples.

"When someone makes fun of me and others laugh, I feel embarrassed. I prefer not to be teased."

"If people never kick the ball to me I feel left out. Please can we make sure everyone gets a turn?"

"When I'm asked to write I panic. I worry about how to start. Please can you help me with the first bit?"

This may look easy on paper, but it takes a lot of practice to get it right. Pupils will get the idea better if this style of communication is modelled consistently within the classroom. When working with a pupil who has a particularly short fuse, it can be helpful to prepare and role play together a script for some of their common trigger points.

When thinking about the anger management difficulties they have, pupils can quickly become defensive. Working with puppets is a useful way of distancing the issue from the pupil to look at it more dispassionately. This is not only helpful with younger children. Secondary pupils can be equally responsive, provided the puppets are used in an age-appropriate way.

There is a wide range of creature puppets on the market that are very useful when considering different responses to threat. Having a selection of these provides potent visual aids in discussions, and some pupils will enjoy using them in role plays. It is worth considering how each creature reacts to threat from others to protect itself, and how it in turn threatens other creatures (if it does). The consequences of their different behaviours can then be considered.

The shark, for example, has a thick skin to protect itself from attack. If it senses itself under threat it tends to attack first. It can attack by thrashing its strong tail or biting with its very sharp teeth. The consequence is that the shark induces great fear in other creatures and is avoided whenever possible. Some people are very aggressive, like the shark – often on the attack.

A bee may fly away if under threat, or may intimidate by circling and buzzing loudly, and ultimately it may sting. However, the consequence of using its ultimate weapon is drastic for the bee as it then dies. In harming another creature, it does even greater harm to itself. If we lose our temper we, like the bee, can be the ones to come off worst.

A snail retreats into its own shell, which serves as good camouflage amongst earth and stones. It does not threaten other creatures so is not feared and is reasonably effective in protecting itself from predators. Taking a low profile and retreating into our shell can sometimes be the best option when we feel unsafe, especially in the classroom.

Spiders can run away fast, roll into a ball to hide, and some 'play dead'. These are effective strategies for escaping danger. Many spiders spin webs to ambush their prey, then sit back and wait for their quarry to be caught. There are people who behave like spiders. They know other people's weak spots and are adept at spinning webs, then sitting back and enjoying the spectacle of their target becoming caught.

Mice run very fast from danger and can even flatten themselves to escape through narrow cracks. They are not easily caught and only bite if cornered or attacked. Mice are very social creatures, often thought of as cute and sometimes kept as pets. They are quite good at keeping themselves safe.

Dragons are mythical creatures from children's story books. They have thick scaly skin that is difficult to penetrate and makes them almost indestructible. With strong claws and sharp teeth, they tear into their prey. But most of all they are renowned for their fearsome roar and the destructive fire they breathe out when roused. The consequence for the dragon is almost always rejection and isolation until, finally, some brave hero deals a fatal blow. The dragon can perhaps be likened to those who intimidate by shouting and swearing, striking fear into those around them. Like the hapless dragon, these people become increasingly isolated and rejected.

It can be interesting to ask a pupil which puppet they see themselves as most like, which their teacher or classmates might say they were like, and which they would most wish to be like. The pros and cons of the various defensive strategies can be discussed with reference to different situations the pupil faces. Younger pupils generally enjoy role playing this with the puppets. If a less aggressive creature is paired with a more aggressive one, the less threatening creature can suggest to the other better ways of behaving to be accepted as a friend. Assertive communication can also be practised through puppet play.

Experiencing some anxiety is normal and can be helpful. In a situation of perceived danger arousal becomes heightened as the body prepares itself to deal with threat. A similar process takes place to that considered in the section on the assault cycle. Anxiety may be accompanied by similar physiological responses to those described for anger. People experience different levels of anxiety in the same situations. Often, the degree of anxiety you experience is related to previous experiences, thoughts, learned coping strategies and modelling by others such as a teacher or parent. Anxiety can help us to maximise our performance, but it can also prevent us from achieving our best or participating fully. For example, feeling anxious can help before an exam or before an interview if it stimulates us in a useful way, such as increasing our ability to focus and raising energy levels. On occasions, however, and for some individuals, anxiety before an exam or interview can be detrimental to performance, making it difficult to focus and reducing energies. It is a matter of degree. If the anxiety becomes too great it can paralyse rational thinking.

Some worries are common to different developmental ages. Babies develop a fear of strangers late in their first year of life. Toddlers experience separation anxiety. Children in infant school often have fears about things that are not based in reality, such as monsters and ghosts. The worries of junior school children tend to reflect real life circumstances such as bodily injury, changes at home or school and natural disasters. In adolescence the focus shifts to relationships, academic results, bodily changes and appearance.

According to the Royal College of Psychiatrists, nearly 300,000 young people in Britain have an anxiety disorder (that is, a level of anxiety that is abnormally high and therefore categorised as a disorder). Anxiety disorders are the most frequent mental disorders in children and adolescents (Beesdo, Knappe and Pine 2009.) The same authors suggest there is evidence to indicate that childhood anxiety can have implications for adult mental health. Childhood anxiety frequently leads to adult depression.

The intervention of choice for supporting those with abnormally high levels of anxiety is CBT. There are cognitive-behavioural programmes that have been developed for use with children in school. The FRIENDS programmes (Fun Friends, Friends for Life, and My Friends Youth) are school-based anxiety prevention and resilience-building programmes, developed in Australia by Dr. Paula Barrett (see Barrett and Randall 2004).

Let's get practical

Schools are recognising that an increasing number of pupils are being hampered by high anxiety. ELSAs often deliver bespoke programmes of support to anxious children and young people. These need to focus on helping them to manage anxiety by challenging their own faulty or exaggerated thinking. Below are some ideas that can be helpful to incorporate into intervention programmes.

Imagine a balloon inside your brain. The more you feed the worry by dwelling on it and adding to the anxious thoughts, the more the balloon inflates. Distracting attention onto more neutral subjects, or challenging the anxious thoughts through cognitive reframing, begins to deflate the balloon. An inflated balloon leaves very little head space for other thoughts, such as school work. A deflated balloon allows head space for other things in your life. This concept could be demonstrated by inflating a balloon in an upturned jar.

A thermometer rating scale could be used to help a child identify the extent to which their anxiety goes up and down, and what makes it better or worse. This can help the child realise they are not worried all the time. They could use it to identify their level of worry before an event, and afterwards to indicate their actual experience of the event, allowing them to see that things are often not as bad as they might have imagined beforehand.

Teaching relaxation and mindfulness can provide children with ways to manage rising anxiety levels for themselves. Choosing to think about happy memories, such as a favourite holiday, or engaging in an enjoyable activity such as reading a book, listening to favourite music or undertaking physical exercise, can provide helpful distractions from thoughts that feed worry.

Some children will be helped by having an object to focus on. Worry dolls are mostly very small hand-made dolls that originate from Guatemala and Mexico. These have traditionally been given to brooding children who would tell their doll about their sorrows, fears and worries, then hide it under their pillow during the night. After this, the child literally sleeps over the whole thing. Next morning, all sorrows are said to have been taken away by the worry doll. These are now often used in our own culture as a special 'listener' for the child. The worry dolls, accessible via the internet, are popular because they are so small and therefore easy to carry around. Similarly, some children are helped by a 'bin it' activity where they write down the current worry, then screw the paper into a ball and throw it in the bin. As they throw it away they choose not to think about it further.

A jar of soothing memories could be made with a child by using a small transparent container and filling it with layers of coloured salt. The salt is coloured by rubbing it with chalks or pastels. While doing this the child thinks of something, someone or somewhere special to them. When the container is full to the brim with salt layers it is sealed so that the layers remain intact even when the container is moved. At bedtime, for example, the child looks at the small jar and remembers the happy thoughts associated with each coloured layer.

Children can be taught positive self-talk, reminding themselves of their strengths and how they have overcome previous difficulties, e.g. 'I usually do better than I think I'm going to,' 'I know how to relax when my muscles get tense,' 'What would Mrs Smith (ELSA) say to me about this?'

While it may be tempting for adults to want to solve children's problems for them, they will become more resilient when they learn to do this for themselves. With support, they can learn step by step problem solving. Below is a six-step model.

1. What is the problem?

2. What could I do?

3. List what might happen

4. Pick the best solution

5. Do it!

6. Did it work?

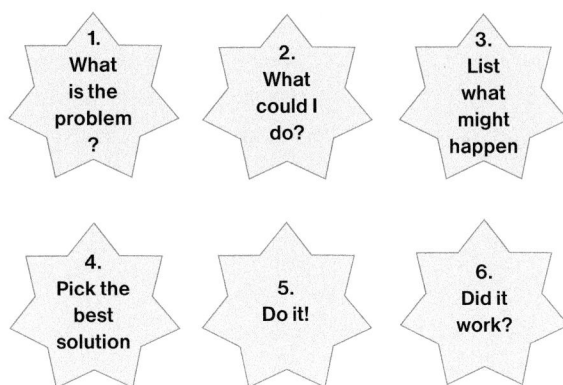

Here is an example of what that might look like.

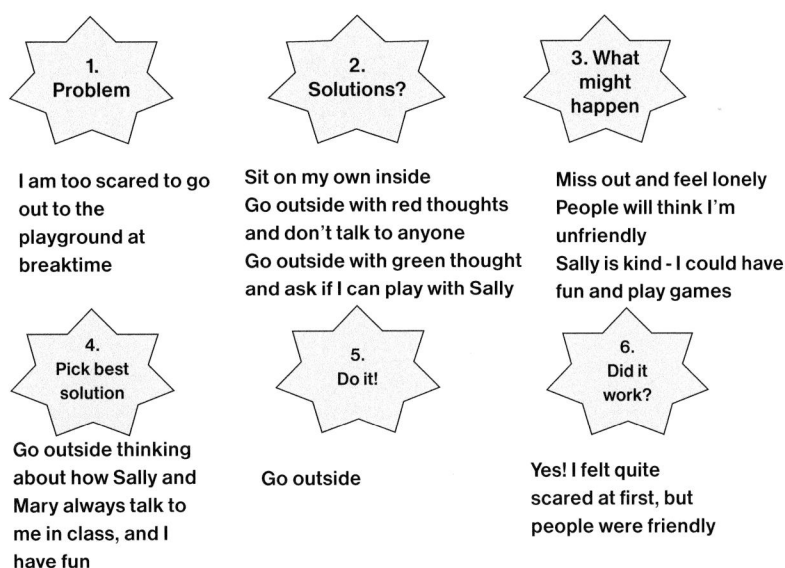

1. Problem

I am too scared to go out to the playground at breaktime

2. Solutions?

Sit on my own inside
Go outside with red thoughts and don't talk to anyone
Go outside with green thought and ask if I can play with Sally

3. What might happen

Miss out and feel lonely
People will think I'm unfriendly
Sally is kind - I could have fun and play games

4. Pick best solution

Go outside thinking about how Sally and Mary always talk to me in class, and I have fun

5. Do it!

Go outside

6. Did it work?

Yes! I felt quite scared at first, but people were friendly

In addition to Paul Stallard's *Think Good - Feel Good* mentioned earlier, three other books that might be particularly useful to school staff supporting anxious children are Laurie Seiler's *Cool Connections with Cognitive Behavioural Therapy* (2008), Huebner and Matthews' *What to Do When You Worry Too Much: A Kid's Guide to Overcoming Anxiety* (2005) and, written particularly with parents in mind, *Overcoming Your Child's Fears and Worries* by Cathy Cresswell and Lucy Willetts (2007).

Summary

The relationship between thoughts, feelings, physiological responses and behaviours (the cognitive-behavioural model) has been explored in relation to managing uncomfortable feelings. We have then focused on two areas of emotional difficulty – anger and anxiety – that are often difficult to manage in school. The assault cycle was used to illustrate the impact of chemicals released into the brain and bloodstream during an angry reaction. A similar physiological response occurs during high anxiety. It is helpful to follow a clear structure when helping pupils to develop more positive anger management skills. The firework model is a very accessible illustration of anger that helps pupils reflect on their behaviour within a framework they can understand. They need patient support if they are to learn that theirs is not the only valid viewpoint in a conflict situation. They also need time and encouragement to explore and experiment with different calming strategies. Cognitive-behavioural approaches are recognised to be an effective way of tackling high anxiety. A variety of practical activities and some useful books have been highlighted to support those working in schools with anxious children.

6. Friendship Skills

Introduction

Most of us have groups of friends that may change over the course of our lives. Changes may occur for a variety of reasons, such as moving to a new house, beginning a new job or starting a new school. Often, we take friendship for granted, expecting it to happen as a natural course of events. Parents, as well, often take it for granted that their children will establish friendships in their school environment, but for some children this is not necessarily the case. Most children at some point in their school careers will go through times of difficulty with friendship and may feel lonely or isolated. For most, this will be a problem that does not last long. But for some the problem can continue and can have long-term effects on their self-esteem and behaviour in school.

Maslow's hierarchy of needs emphasises how we all need to belong or feel part of a group. When pupils feel that they do not belong and feel they are not liked or accepted by their peers, they usually respond in one of two ways. They may isolate themselves, withdrawing from others, rarely initiating conversations and wandering by themselves at break times rather than trying to interact. Such pupils are often described as 'acting in'. Alternatively, they may make it their mission to be noticed by others and so engage in attention-seeking or perhaps disruptive behaviour. Such pupils are often described as 'acting out'. Using a questionnaire that asks pupils to identify who they enjoy spending time with and who they find it difficult to spend time with, can give us insights into the friendship dynamics that exist within a class. Some pupils may receive many nominations of being difficult to work with from their peers; these individuals are described as being rejected (Asher and Coie 1990). Other pupils may receive very few nominations of friendship from their peers. It is not that they are disliked; it is simply that they are overlooked. These individuals are often described as being neglected rather than rejected. A study by Coie and Kupersmidt (1983) showed there was a close relationship between unprovoked aggression and rejected status. The question of course is which comes first, the unprovoked aggression or the rejected status?

Whatever the cause of social isolation, and it is likely to be a combination of factors, the consequences are wide ranging. Pupils who experience rejection during primary school are more likely to truant and achieve poorly at secondary school (Frederickson 1991); they are also more likely to experience mental health problems in later life (Cowen et al 1973).

What can you do to help?

There are several ways that school staff can help to facilitate positive friendships for pupils who are isolated. The key is to bring them into a circle of support and give them opportunities for interaction to help friendships develop. This might involve putting them in a group for project work or putting in place a friendship group intervention whereby a group of pupils meet each week for building friendship skills. The 'Circle of Friends' intervention has been adapted and used in a variety of ways, two of which are described in this chapter. There is evidence to suggest that the intervention can be helpful for improving social interactions and social acceptance as well as developing empathy. Research suggests that often the intervention is more successful in changing the attitude of peers rather than changing the target child's behaviour per se. It has also been found to be beneficial for young people with autism (Barrett and Randall 2004; Frederickson, Warren and Turner 2005; Newton, Taylor and Wilson 1996; O'Connor 2016; Shotton, 1998; Whitaker et al 1998).

Setting up a circle of friends

'Circle of friends' was originally developed by Pearpoint, Forest and Snow (1992) to set up a support network around an individual who is isolated. Two methods for setting up a circle of friends are described here. You will need to use your professional judgement, consulting with colleagues, carers and the pupil, to know which would be more helpful. As Robson (2000) notes, when evaluating social programmes it is useful to ask, 'What works best for whom under what circumstances?'

Method 1 (The target pupil is identified to the rest of the class)

(This method may be more suited to pupils who are 'acting out' rather than 'acting in'.)

1. Ask the target pupil for their permission for the procedure to go ahead, explaining what it will entail and for a circle of friends to be set up. Ask them who they would like to be in the circle of friends group, who they would like to get to know better.

2. Obtain permission from the parents outlining the procedure to them.

3. With the target pupil *not present*, talk to the whole class. Explain that this is a very special lesson and you are going to do something that you do not normally do, i.e. talk about someone when they are not there, but because of the difficulties that this pupil has been having you need their help.

4. Establish some ground rules; for example:

   • When someone is talking we listen

   • No put downs or dirty looks

   • Information is confidential.

5. Brainstorm: What does the target pupil do? Record the results on a flip chart.

6. Brainstorm: Some positive things they have noticed about the target pupil.

7. Give out the circles exercise (see sheet with concentric circles) explaining how they should fill it in.

   • Circle 1: Write the names of people who you are closest to in your life (usually family members).

- Circle 2: People who are close friends but not quite as close as circle 1.

- Circle 3: Acquaintances, people who you know to say hello to or chat to superficially at clubs or school.

- Circle 4: People paid to be in your life such as teachers, doctors, hairdressers etc.

8. Ask them to cross out all the people who are in circles 2 and 3. Imagine they no longer exist.

9. Ask them how it would *feel* if their life looked like this? Record their responses onto a flip chart.

10. Ask how they would *act* if their lives were like this? Record their responses on a flip chart.

11. Compare their responses with those produced by the class about the target pupil. Are there any similarities? Often at this point the children make the connection between the target pupil's behaviour and their lack of friends.

12. Brainstorm: What can we do to help the target pupil? List ideas on a flip chart.

13. Outline how we need a special group to work with the target pupil to help them get back on track and make friends. We need five to seven volunteers to meet with the target pupil and a teacher/TA once per week. Ask them to indicate on their circles sheet if they would like to be part of the group, or alternatively ask volunteers to raise their hand.

14. From the list of willing participants and the list of pupils that the target pupil identified as being people they would like to get to know better, choose a group of five to seven pupils. The key here is to choose a group of pupils with whom the target pupil will be able to relate and perhaps establish friendships. Some of the other pupils may also have friendship needs.

Method 2 (Target pupil not identified and remains anonymous)

1. Ask the target pupil for their permission for the procedure to go ahead, explaining what it will entail, and for a circle of friends to be set up. Ask them who they would like to be in the circle of friends group, who they would like to get to know better.

2. Obtain permission from the parents, outlining the procedure to them.

3. With the target pupil *present* talk to the whole class. Establish some ground rules, for example:

- When someone is talking we listen

- No put downs or dirty looks

- Information is confidential.

4. Talk about the importance of friendships and how all of us at some point in our lives will feel lonely or left out.

5. Give out circles exercise (see sheet with concentric circles) and explain how to fill it in.

- Circle 1: Write the names of people who you are closest to in your life (usually family members).

- Circle 2: People who are close friends but not quite as close as circle 1.

- Circle 3: Acquaintances, people who you know to say hello to or chat to superficially at clubs, school.

- Circle 4: People paid to be in your life such as teachers, doctors, hairdressers etc.

6. Ask them to cross out all the people who are in circles 2 and 3. Imagine they no longer exist.

7. Brainstorm: How would you *feel* if your life looked like this? Record their responses onto a flip chart.

8. Brainstorm: How would you *act* if your life looked like this? Record their responses on a flip chart.

9. Explain that you are going to be setting up a special group for people to get to know one another better and become better friends. It will meet once per week with (name of staff member). Ask who would like to be part of the group. They can either indicate on their circles sheet or put their hand up. You will usually find that most pupils want to be part of the group.

10. From the list of willing participants and the list of pupils that the target pupil identified as being people they would like to get to know better, choose a group of five to seven pupils. The key here is to choose a group of pupils with whom the target pupil will be able to relate and perhaps establish friendships. Some of the other pupils may also have friendship needs.

Circle of friends

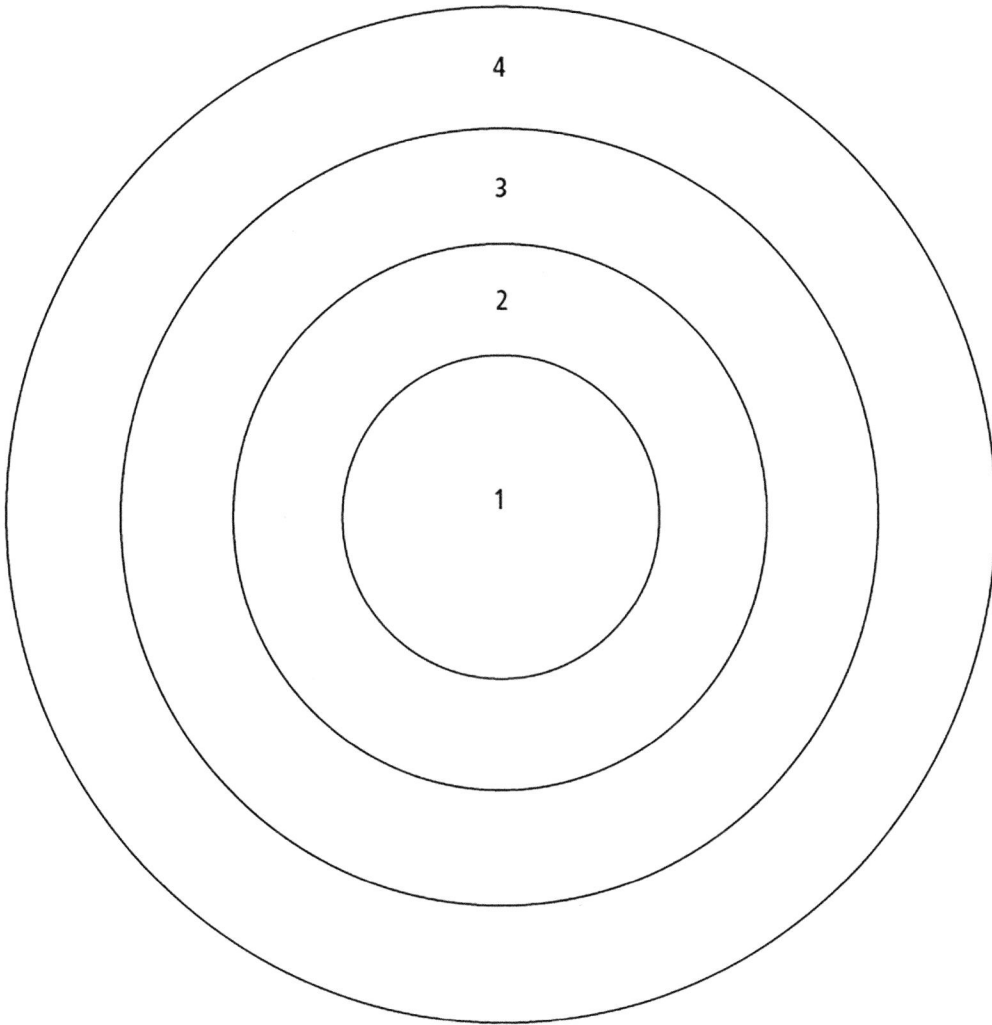

4

3

2

1

You can set up a friendship group without using the Circle of Friends procedures described previously. This can be just one group that focuses on developing the relationships within that group or it can be across a class. In some schools every member of a class is in a small friendship group that meets once a week with an adult facilitating. This obviously has time and personnel implications but, in many ways, is the most inclusive option. Giving everyone in the class an opportunity to have small group time each week where they have an opportunity to talk and develop friendship/social skills is valuable experience.

The group meetings

These can take place at any time according to the needs of the adult taking the group and timetable restraints. Some groups run very successfully as part of the Personal, Social and Health Education (PSHE) time; others meet during lunch times or curriculum time. The group meetings should happen at the same time and place each week in order to help the pupils remember to attend regularly. A suitable room where everyone feels comfortable, and where there are going to be minimal interruptions, is also important. Having some display space available in the room is also an advantage.

Content of the sessions

The sessions should follow a familiar format each week:

1. Start each week with the group aims: Why are we here?

    • To help one another become better friends

    • To learn how we can help one another at school.

2. Establish some ground rules. Ask them to make their own ground rules for the group so that they take ownership of them. Do not let them make too many though! Generally speaking, you only want three or four. These might be along the lines of:

    i.) When someone speaks we look and listen

    ii.) What is said in the room stays in the room (unless it is something where the teacher feels you might be in some danger)

    iii.) No put downs or dirty looks.

    Go over the ground rules at the beginning of each session. This helps members of the group to feel secure.

3. Warm up activity/ice breaker

    Circle Time warm up games are useful here, e.g. pass the keys round the circle without them making a sound. The type of warm up/ice breaker that you chose will depend on the age of the pupils. See Circle Time books for more ideas.

4. Review of the week

    You might ask them to share one thing that has gone well this week and one thing that has not gone so well.

5. Focus activity

This might be about getting to know one another better, how to give and receive information, conflict resolution, giving and receiving compliments etc. Games and puppets are very useful here.

6. Task for the week

    How can we support one another this week in the playground or classroom? This might be agreeing to give Johnny a nudge to remind him to put his hand up rather than shout out, or looking out for Katrina in the playground as she always seems to end up on her own etc.

7. To help establish a group identity ask the members to make up a name for their group. You might also like to take a photo of the group.

8. Usually at the end of the session have juice and biscuits. The pupils look forward to this part of the group and it can be a real incentive for coming. Giving them this extra privilege of having a snack in school can be extremely nurturing and, if you get them to take turns to serve one another and insist on good manners, it forms a useful opportunity for social skills training as well. At the end of the session remind them of the next time and place you will be meeting.

9. At the end of an appropriate length of time (e.g. six weeks), it is a good idea to give out certificates. These could mark the end of a group or they might just be an encouragement for the group to celebrate all they have learned so far and how much they have become better friends because of the group.

When should groups end?

Groups can finish when the participants no longer need the support of the group or when it is felt that the group is not meeting the needs that it was set up for. It is worth saying that sometimes some groups just do not work; the members just do not seem to gel. The failure of the group may not be due to inadequate planning or preparation but simply because of the group dynamics, the mix of pupils within the group. Just chalk it up to experience and get on with your next group; chances are that this one will be more successful!

Some groups can be challenging to manage. They do not seem to listen to one another or take the tasks seriously. A useful and positive way of improving their focus on listening is to have the incentive of a listening certificate. This is given out each week at the end to the pupil who displays the best listening behaviour. Remind them that good listening behaviour means looking at the person who is speaking and staying quiet until they have finished. Keeping a tally of when you see this behaviour from each pupil means that you can see whether their listening behaviour is improving over the weeks and means you can fairly identify the best listener for that week. Many pupils have said the most valuable thing they had learnt was how to listen to others!

Pupil	Listening behaviour tally
John	IIII
Simon	II
Phillip	III
Joshua	I
Fen	III

Poor behaviour should not be simply ignored but you need to use the least intrusive strategy to begin with. A good first step is to refer non-verbally to the rules by pointing at the appropriate rule that is on display (a good reason to always have the rules on display). If the disruption continues you may give a verbal rules reminder, 'John, what was the rule we made about listening?' If difficulties continue then it is useful to remind the pupil that they chose to be part of the group but their behaviour is telling you that they are not ready to be part of the group today. If they continue to flout the rules they will be asked to leave. If indeed they do continue you must follow through and ask them to leave the group for this week. You can arrange to talk to them later about what went wrong and what they need to do next time.

Summary

At some point in their lives most children experience difficulties with friendships. For some children these difficulties are long term and can have a lasting impact on their self-esteem and behaviour in school. Circle of Friends is a useful intervention for helping to build a group of friends around an isolated individual. A circle of friends can be set up either by openly identifying the pupil's needs to the other pupils or by keeping the target pupil anonymous and simply building a friendship circle without openly identifying it is particularly for the needs of that pupil. Sensitivity and guidance from the pupil themselves are key in deciding which approach to take. Running friendship skills groups is another strategy for helping children learn how to make and keep friends.

7. Therapeutic stories

Introduction

Therapeutic stories are narratives that help children and young people discover there are solutions to their worries and problems. Through listening to a story of someone who has been through a difficult yet similar situation to themselves, individuals can be encouraged to discover positive strategies that might work for them. Stories can also help them to feel that they are not the only one who has experienced a particular difficulty, so that they feel less alone.

When we read or listen to a story we often take on the perspective of the characters in the story. Neuro-imaging research supports this idea. Studies have found that when people read a sentence about a person performing an action, the same regions of the brain are activated as actually performing that action (Buccino et al 2005; Glenberg, Satao and Cattaneo 2008). Studies have also shown changes in how we see ourselves as a result of reading fiction (e.g. Djikic and Oatley 2014). Research suggests that reading fiction helps us to identify with and understand others better, thus increasing our levels of empathy (Kidd and Castano 2013; Mar, Oatley and Peterson 2009). As well as increasing empathy, there is evidence to suggest that stories have the power to influence changes in our behaviour, such as increased altruism and pro-social behaviour as well as decreases in prejudice (Johnson 2012, 2013).

Stories can help individuals view their difficulties from a different point of view, recognising and acknowledging their behaviour where they may have been unwilling to do so before. The story might also open up to them why they have behaved in a particular way and help them appreciate how their behaviour may have impacted upon others. This increased awareness, as well as the comfort, hope and knowledge of strategies, can give the child or young person the courage they need for positive change to occur.

Using stories to influence and change individuals is nothing new. Throughout generations and across cultures and religions, stories have been used in this way. Every society has its own collection of folk tales, myths and legends that have been used to educate, impart values and change attitudes or beliefs. Aesop, writing in the mid-6th century BC in ancient Greece, often used animal characters to help educate and communicate a moral message. There is a very useful website where you can read over many of Aesop's fables online. The moral for each one is often included and many of the fables are also available to listen to: www.aesopfables.com.

Bruno Bettelheim wrote about the value of certain stories for children's emotional development. In his book 'The Uses of Enchantment', he compares telling stories to scattering seeds, only some of which would germinate and grow in the mind of the child. The seeds would remain undisturbed until the child's mind had reached a state suitable for their germination.

Doris Brett is a clinical psychologist who has written two books, 'Annie Stories' (1986) and 'More Annie Stories' (1992). The texts are aimed at parents, encouraging them to use stories to help their children. In the books she provides a number of stories that parents can adapt for their child according to the particular difficulty the child is having. A variety of topics are covered, such as the birth of a sibling, starting school for the first time and the death of a loved one. Each story is about a little girl called Annie, hence the titles. The idea is that parents will change the name of the child in the story to be similar, but not the same, as that of their own child. The story the parents tell should reflect the worries or difficulties faced by their own child, but the child in the story finds strategies to help them deal with their worries and difficulties.

As well as parents using this approach it is also suitable for staff to use in schools with troubled and troubling pupils. The stories that are written do not limit the hero/heroine to always being a child of a similar age and name as the target pupil. Depending on the interests of the pupil, sometimes the hero or heroine can be a dinosaur, a footballer, a car, a dragon or a mechanic, to name but a few examples.

Denial

Pupils often find it difficult to admit to having committed unfair acts (as do we all). They find it difficult to admit both to themselves or anyone else that what they have done is wrong or that it might have hurt someone in some way. They do not want to think about it and being overtly confronted with their behaviour often sends them further into denial, as they blatantly refuse to take responsibility and acknowledge their behaviour. They become very good at justifying their behaviour to themselves: 'What I did was not so bad. No one really got hurt.' Alternatively, they avoid thinking about it at all, as it is easier not to. A story is a non-threatening way of helping a pupil reflect upon their behaviour and look at it from a different perspective.

Using a cognitive behavioural perspective

Prochaska and DiClemente (1982) present six stages that an individual may go through in changing their behaviour. The first stage is called the pre-contemplative stage. Here the individual sees no problem with their behaviour but knows that others disapprove. The second stage is only reached when the individual becomes willing to accept that their behaviour *may be* problematic and that change might be desirable. Sometimes helping a pupil to move from stage one to stage two can be very difficult (for more detail on the stages of change model, Eddie McNamara has written a very readable summary in his publication '*Motivational Interviewing*' (1998)).

A story can be used to help a pupil move from stage one to stage two. The story allows the pupil to examine and reflect on their behaviour in a non-confrontational way and consider the disadvantages of their behaviour. The story can also present alternative strategies to the pupil that they can use in specific situations, outlining to them how such strategies could be successful. Using the story may also help the pupil to move to stage three of the Prochaska and DiClemente stages of change model. At this stage the pupil makes the decision to cease engaging in the problematic behaviour and start engaging in positive behaviour instead.

William was a year one child whose behaviour was causing great concern in school. Often in response to being asked to do something he would hide, run out of class, kick or hurt others. A behaviour support worker was put in place to try to help the situation and the following story was used to help William make sense of the intervention, as well as helping to clarify the reasons for his extreme behaviour when being asked to do something in class.

Case study (continued)

Walter learns to enjoy school

Walter was a little boy who lived at home with his mummy and younger brother, Tony. Walter was interested in dinosaurs. He could tell you all about the different types of dinosaurs that used to live on earth.

Walter went to school. Sometimes at school he had got into lots of trouble and everyone had been very cross with him.

Sometimes his mummy had had to come into school and take him home.

You see, when the teacher asked him to draw or write something, Walter didn't want to do it. He would shout, 'No, I don't want to!'

Sometimes he would run away and hurt other children or damage classroom displays. Why do you think Walter didn't want to write or draw?

Was he afraid of not doing it right?

Was he afraid that everyone would laugh at him if he didn't get it *just* right?

Was he afraid of his teacher getting cross with him if he didn't get it right?

Perhaps there was another reason. What do you think?

Then one day, after a holiday, Mrs Harper came to school. She was going to be Walter's helper. Mrs Harper worked with Walter on his own table away from the other children. This helped Walter to concentrate on his work.

Having a helper was great because then Walter knew that even if the work looked really difficult, there would be someone there to help him.

When he was asked to do something Walter stopped saying,

'No, I don't want to!' and started to say, 'Yes, I'll have a try.'

And do you know, when Walter tried, he found that he could often do the work, and do it very well?

Everyone was really pleased with him for having a try. And Walter was then allowed to put another piece on his dinosaur puzzle, which he loved to do!

His helper, Mrs Harper was pleased!

His teacher, Mrs Turner was pleased!

Mrs Potter, the head teacher was pleased!

And his mummy was really pleased!

Walter felt really happy. It was much nicer to try hard in school than to say, 'No, I don't want to!'

Walter began to enjoy going to school more and more. In fact, at the end of each day he said to his mummy that he didn't want to go home!

Comfort and release

It is comforting to hear a story about someone who has gone through a similar difficulty to yourself. Through hearing such stories pupils feel that they are not alone. It is helpful to know there are others who understand and have experienced what they are feeling. They might have also behaved in a similar, perhaps irrational way, even if their behaviour is not completely identical. All of this knowledge can bring comfort and release to the pupil. They feel understood and accepted rather than feeling abnormal and judged.

Hearing about new strategies

Stories allow advice to be given or strategies to be shared in a less directive way. I'm sure we have all felt annoyed by someone who has given us the benefit of their wisdom when it was not asked for. In such situations pupils often feel judged, threatened and angry, however good or well-meaning the advice. This is particularly the case for pupils who have little self-esteem to begin with and so feel the need to defend themselves from what they perceive as attacks. They cannot afford to take any chances, perhaps because they have already had so many experiences where others have put them down or hurt them in the past. Consequently, when someone tries to help them with useful advice, their defences go up. Their internal working model interprets the situation in the following way: 'By giving me this advice you're saying I'm stupid and that you know better than me, ' and so the information is likely to be rejected.

A story is a much less threatening way to receive information or advice. In a story no one is judging the pupil or telling them what they should do. The pupil is simply finding out about someone else who has been through something similar and found a way of dealing with it that might also work for them. It is then up to them whether they subsequently change their behaviour, but at least through hearing how someone else has managed their feelings effectively and dealt with a similar situation, they know of some strategies that might also work for them. At this point they then have a choice, whereas before they may have felt trapped in a cycle of behaviour that they could see no way out of.

A consistent approach

Stories not only work to help the pupil involved, they can also help parents, carers and teachers to know how an intervention is meant to work and how they can support the pupil when they are trying out new strategies. In this way positive behaviour can be reinforced more effectively, making the process of change more likely to happen. It should be acknowledged that changing your behaviour is often not an easy thing to do (as any ex-smoker will tell you) especially when habits are ingrained over years. Pupils need encouragement from all the key adults involved, and the adults need to understand their role in providing the right kind of encouragement. A story can help the adults as well as the pupil to understand the sorts of things that they can do to help, and consequently the intervention is more likely to be a success.

Developing an understanding of the pupil

To write a successful story, you need to understand some of the underlying reasons for the pupil's behaviour, or at least develop some hypotheses. You can then partly write a story and then work in partnership with the pupil to finish it. Alternatively, you can write a story with questions embedded in the text in order to explore their responses and test your hypotheses, as in the story 'Walter learns to enjoy school'.

Here are a number of questions that were asked within the context of the story to explore the child's view of why the character in the story did not want to write.

- Why do you think Walter didn't want to write or draw?

- Was he afraid of not doing it right?

- Was he afraid that everyone would laugh at him if he didn't get it just right?

- Was he afraid of his teacher getting cross with him if he didn't get it right?

- Perhaps there was another reason. What do you think?

When a child responds with ideas, he is likely to be revealing something of himself.

You also need to find out more about the pupil; who they admire as well as what motivates and interests them. Do they love football and worship a particular player or are they interested in car mechanics or ice skating or animals? If the story is going to capture the pupil's imagination and attention it needs to contain characters or activities that they are interested in.

What age range can stories be used with?

We have used stories with pupils ranging from 3 to 14 years old. The way the story is written, and the type and number of illustrations used, obviously varies tremendously, but as long as you stick with the genre and language of the particular age group there is no reason why therapeutic stories cannot be used with a wide range of ages.

Case study

A story for an older pupil

This story was written for a year nine student who had some difficulties managing his feelings in certain situations. He could keep himself under control in some situations but tended to overreact if he perceived himself as being blamed unjustly when others were involved or had triggered incidents.

Kit's short fuse

'But it *wasn't* me!' insisted Kit, his head beginning to throb. 'You always think it's *my* fault!' His voice was getting louder and higher. Fists clenched, he walked towards the teacher, staring her out. He was starting to swear now; he knew he shouldn't, but he just couldn't stop himself. '*OUT*!' she shouted back at him. 'Get out of my lesson *now*!' Kit was glad to oblige – he was going anyway.

Out in the corridor he paced up and down; he banged his fist on the wall a few times. *Ouch*. Slowly some of the tension began to drain away, but the anger remained. He'd done a lot to turn his behaviour round but one thing still made him mad every time. It was so unfair. Teachers were too quick to blame him. If he'd done it then 'fair cop', but when he hadn't … that was so out of order.

He turned the incident over and over in his mind. He had a right to be angry. But now another thought was pressing in on him. He'd done it – he'd *really* done it. Now there'd be trouble. Miss Crofter, deputy head, had told him often enough, 'If you swear at teachers, Kit, we have to put you out. You know the rules. It's an automatic exclusion.'

And it was. Three days this time. The more it happened the longer they got. And in some ways, Miss Crofter was the least of his worries. His mum's reaction was worse – much worse. She always tightened the screw.

No money. No treats. Kit was grounded. He wasn't allowed out; friends weren't allowed in. He couldn't even sit in front of the telly all day – exclusions came with work to be done these days.

And when that was finished, his mum always had some extra chores! It was no picnic being at home, that was for sure. Then, as if all day with Mum wasn't enough, he had little sister to look forward to. She really knew how to get on his nerves!

It would usually start off OK. Lucy liked him being around. She liked to join in his computer games. She wasn't bad either – except she couldn't stand him winning. Trouble was, he mostly did. She'd whinge a bit, then go off in a sulk. Mum was always telling Kit to let her win, just because she was younger than him. But what was the point of playing if you didn't try to win?

The thing that really got him, though, was the way Lucy helped herself to his CDs and never put them back. And now she'd done it again. The one he wanted was missing; Kit was livid. He marched off to her room. 'Give it here,' he demanded, 'Give me my CD!' Lucy denied all knowledge. 'I *know* it's you,' said Kit. 'It's *always* you!' And that was it. That's all it took. She shouted. She stamped. She screamed. 'It's *not fair*! You always blame me. I haven't *had* your rotten CD!' Then came the tears.

Kit had seen it all before. When would she grow up? He'd only asked for his CD back. It wasn't long of course before Mum appeared at the door of his room. 'What have you done to Lucy?' 'I haven't done anything to Lucy,' Kit protested. 'She's nicked one of my CDs again.' 'How do you know it was her?' his mum asked. 'Because it's always her!' he replied.

Mum was looking round his room. 'What's that under your chair?' she asked, pointing. 'Is that the one?' Oh dear. He hadn't seen it there. Yes, that was the one. 'I think you owe your sister an apology,' Mum continued. 'I don't know why she got into such a state,' Kit complained. 'I thought it was her … it nearly always is.' 'Perhaps she doesn't like being accused of things she hasn't done,' his mum replied, '… and I think I know someone else like that!'

She had a point. Perhaps Lucy wasn't the only one who needed to get things into perspective.

A staged approach for successful story writing

In her book, '*Annie Stories*', Doris Brett provides a useful set of guidelines for making up stories. An adapted version of this list is shown below.

1. Think about the difficulty that has created the need for a story. How might the pupil be feeling? Try to put yourself in their shoes.

2. What ideas do you want to communicate to the pupil through the vehicle of the story? What sort of solutions or resolutions do you want to suggest?

3. Start the story with a hero or heroine who has similar fears or difficulties to the pupil.

4. The plot should reflect the difficulties the pupil is facing but then go on to suggest a positive solution for the hero or heroine.

5. Be sensitive to any comments or questions the pupil asks as you read the story. It is often interesting to turn the question back to the pupil and ask them, 'Well what do you think?' This can give you valuable insights into how they are thinking.

6. If you are not sure why the pupil is feeling worried in a particular situation, use questions in the story to find out, such as, 'Why do you think Henry was worried about that? What did Henry think might happen?'

7. If the pupil tries out a solution suggested in the story and it does not work, do not worry. Find out what they did and then create a story about the hero or heroine who also tried that particular solution and it did not work, but then went on to find something that did work.

8. Keep the vocabulary and length of the story appropriate to the child's age and attention span.

The pupil has read the story. What should I do next?

There are a number of options once the pupil has read the story. You can give them their own personal copy, or better still give them one with room for illustrations. Some pupils are extremely motivated to illustrate their story on the computer using clip art. If they are unable to read their story independently you could record it for them to listen to at home. Or liaise closely with parents for them to share it with the pupil at home. If the pupil is a good reader another idea to get them to interact with the story is to ask them to read and record it for other listeners, or ask them to read it to a less able peer or younger child.

Resist the temptation to demand an interpretation of the story. If you have got the content right it will resonate with the pupil, but change may not be immediate. It is useful to think of Bettelheim's analogy that telling stories is like scattering seeds: some of them may lie dormant for some time before they start to grow, others may grow immediately and still others may not grow at all. Asking more general questions such as, 'What did you think of the story?' can sometimes be helpful, or asking what they thought of a particular character or what they thought of what the hero did etc.

It will depend very much on the age and character of the pupil as to how many times the story is read and used. If a pupil finds a story relevant, helpful, or comforting to them in some way then they will come back to it. Often, they bring it up in conversation or ask for it to be read again. However, if they do not mention it again do not feel you have failed. It is perhaps the case that the pupil did not relate to the character in the story or perhaps the story was a little too close to the truth for comfort and they were not yet ready to face their feelings and behaviour. What cannot be underestimated is the impact that writing a story can have on a pupil's self-esteem. Knowing that you spent the time and effort creating a story especially for them helps to communicate your care for them and how important you think they are.

Summary

Therapeutic stories can work to help troubled or troubling pupils on a number of levels. They are based on characters that have something in common with the target pupil. Stories can help them, in an unobtrusive way, to feel comfort and reassurance, recognise their own behaviour and learn about possible strategies for managing the challenges they experience in ways that reduce their troubling behaviour. Creating a story for a pupil is a useful exercise in itself for helping you to think about whether you have fully understood what is going on for them.

8. Social skills

Introduction

To belong to and relate to others is a fundamental human need. We are social beings, born with an innate need to interact with others. Colwyn Trevarthen (professor of child psychology and psychobiology at the University of Edinburgh) is a leading researcher into the early social behaviour of infants. In a video we used in earlier ELSA training, he demonstrated that even tiny babies engage in reciprocal 'conversations' with their parents. They know to pause and wait for a response from their parent to the sounds and movements that they make. Parent and child engage in a kind of conversational dance as they respond in turn to each other. It is likely that this early interaction paves the way to the development of good communication between parent and child, then child and others.

We have referred several times to Maslow's hierarchy of needs. After physiological and safety needs comes the need for a sense of belonging. This is normally first established within the family, but as the child grows the peer group becomes increasingly important. That sense of belonging contributes crucially to the development of good self-esteem, discussed in chapter 4. Yet for many children in school the basic skills underlying successful social interaction have not been learned and so will need to be specifically taught. The acquisition of skills is influenced by the example of others. While the impulse to relate may be innate, the process of interaction is largely learned. Motivation is an important stimulus for initiating interaction and will sometimes be less and other times be greater, dependent upon individual needs and interests. Feedback from others is an important contributor to the development and retention of new social skills.

Why communicate?

Before embarking on social skills training programmes, it is helpful to stop and think why social communication is so important to us. Schutz (1988) identified three basic elements that motivate our need to communicate:

- **Identity** – we seek a sense of belonging, accompanied by feelings of involvement and acknowledgement.

- **Control** – we want to be able to initiate action and respond to others, as well as determine who we speak to and what we say.

- **Acceptance** – we want to make friends, fit in socially with others and be liked.

The nature of communication

Social communication has a purpose. When we communicate, it is for specific reasons. Often these may be to obtain something we need such as information or assistance, but it may also be to help another. We exercise a degree of choice over the timing and nature of interactions according to our interest or needs at any given moment. We are also able to adapt our communication to suit the situation. The way we speak to a teacher or stranger differs from the way we speak to a friend. A casual chat has a different style from speaking in a formal group, such as a school assembly.

Communication is much more, however, than the words we say. It has been suggested that body language contributes the major part of information communicated in any face to face encounter. This is done through posture, gestures, movements and facial expressions. The next largest component of spoken communication may be the tone and modulation of the voice together with the pace of speech. Perhaps it is only a small percentage of what we say that is communicated by the actual words used. This is, of course, difficult to measure.

The greater importance of *how* we say something over the actual words used can be demonstrated in a simple exercise involving changing emphasis. The following sentence can be put onto seven separate cards, with a different word written in italics each time to denote emphasis:

I didn't say she stole my purse.

This exercise works particularly well in a group but could also be done as a paired activity when an adult is working individually with a pupil. After each card is read, the implied meaning is discussed. 'I didn't *say* she stole my purse' means something quite different from 'I didn't say *she* stole my purse.' Changing which word in the sentence is emphasised gives seven different likely meanings to this one apparently simple sentence.

We live in an age of increasing communication via social media. Texts, messages and emails comprise words and punctuation only. They may be written with one tone of voice in mind, but be read with another entirely. For this reason, they can sometimes lead to misunderstanding and offence. The implication of this is that learning to use body language and voice tone well is vital to effective social communication. The importance of the feedback gained from body posture and facial gestures can be experienced by having two people sit back to back in chairs while they hold a conversation. They have no visual cues about how their partner is receiving the information they are sharing, or whether their partner wishes to take a turn in the conversation.

Basic social communication skills

In their Social Skills Handbook, Hutchings, Comins and Offiler (1991) list 13 basic skills underpinning social communication:

- Eye contact – when we look at another person in the eyes and the gaze is returned.

- Facial expression – the basic expressions of anger, fear, disgust, happiness, sadness and surprise have been identified as universal across cultures.

- Gestures – such as nodding or shaking the head, finger wagging, hand and arm movements used to add emphasis or indicate size, direction etc.

- Posture – conveying, for example, tension, interest and relaxation.

- Proximity – the amount of 'personal space' between one person and another.

- Touch – physical contact conveying reassurance, comfort, joy, congratulation etc.

- Appearance – this may be used, for example, to reflect personality, status, group belonging or attitude.

- Listening – paying attention. Active listening involves a high level of concentration and making appropriate responses.

- Initiating a relationship – establishing a common interest and exploring compatibility.

- Developing a relationship – usually based on involvement in mutual activities, shared interests, attitudes and values.

- Self-disclosure – sharing personal information, opinions or feelings.

- Empathy – being able to put yourself in another person's shoes and see things from their point of view, even if it is different from your own.

- Positive regard – treating another person with respect regardless of difference or disagreement.

A staged approach to teaching social skills

Crucial to our consideration here is the knowledge that social skills can be improved through support, practice and encouragement. To do this, the necessary skills need to be identified and broken down into manageable steps for learning. As in all aspects of emotional literacy, good social skills need to be modelled by those working with a pupil, not just taught. Pupils learn more from the way we are than the things we say. The pupil needs an example to emulate and opportunities for practice.

Let us imagine that you want to prepare a pupil to be part of a duty rota for looking after the reception desk during lunch break. They will need to learn how to greet visitors to the school and answer the telephone. The component skills need to be identified. First there is the need for **demonstration**, either by watching it done for real or through role play. Perhaps you show the pupil how to say hello, introduce themselves and ask if they can help. Then they have a go themselves. Initially during this **practice** stage, you offer **guidance** to help them get it right, then you give them opportunity to practise unprompted until they are confident. You give positive **feedback**, praising their achievements so that their new skills are reinforced and remembered. Then you introduce the next skill, which may be asking the visitor for his name and asking him to take a seat while the pupil finds the member of staff he needs to see. Again, you follow the stages of demonstration, practice, guidance and feedback. When the component skills have been learned, the pupil practises putting them together into a seamless sequence.

Let's get practical

Most pupils learn better through experience than by simply being told. When supporting pupils to develop particular social skills, we will be more effective if we provide memorable learning experiences. Various ideas for learning activities, related to some of the basic skills that have been listed in this chapter, are presented below. Some of these will be suitable for two people working together while others will work well in a group.

Eye contact

Mutual eye gaze signals interest and a willingness to interact further. It usually lasts about a second. If we do not want to talk, we look away. For example, in a situation of enforced proximity such as a lift, we may look down or fix our gaze on the buttons to avoid interaction. Appropriate eye contact between two strangers tends to follow the pattern of brief eye contact, looking away briefly before making eye contact again to establish either an interested or disinterested response to communicating by the other party.

The importance of eye contact to conversation can be demonstrated by having two people engage in conversation, with one taking the role of speaker and the other listener. The speaker talks on a subject of their choice (e.g. a favourite holiday, their pets, what they did at the weekend). Initially the listener fails to give the speaker any eye contact. After a minute, the listener looks at the speaker's face while she talks for a further minute. The pair could then swap roles and repeat the exercise. They then discuss how it felt to talk when the listener refused to look at them. Often the talker finds they dry up or lose their train of thought.

In a group, secret instruction cards can be used. Two children are chosen to take the roles of speaker and listener. The listener draws a card from the secret instruction card pack and follows the instruction while the speaker talks to them. Instructions could include:

- Stare at the speaker

- Don't look at the speaker's face

- From time to time check your watch

- Look through the pages of a book

- Keep glancing out of the window.

The task for the other members of the group is to guess the instruction on the card. Once guessed, the speaker can say how that behaviour affected them.

Eye contact can be very uncomfortable for some pupils, especially those on the autistic spectrum or those who are particularly shy. Such pupils can be taught to focus on another area of the speaker's face, such as the ear or end of the nose. It will appear to the speaker that they have eye contact while being more comfortable and sustainable for the listener.

Facial expression

Researchers have identified six primary facial expressions, although there are degrees of each. These are anger, fear, disgust, happiness, sadness and surprise. Excessive use of facial expression can be distracting within communication, while lack of expression can be disarming. Facial expressions need to match the emotional tone of the conversation or situation. In school, children are sometimes seen to smile when being told off. While often assumed to indicate disrespect, it may instead indicate nervousness or embarrassment.

Have a set of photo cards reflecting different emotions. Create a set of situation cards to match these emotions. These could be pictorial scenarios for younger children while written scenarios for secondary age pupils would be adequate. The pupil is asked to choose a suitable facial expression to match each situation card. For example, a small child treading in dog mess and walking it into the hall carpet may be matched to cards depicting disgust or anger, but smiling or laughter would not be appropriate. An extension to this activity could be to copy that facial expression while looking at yourself in a small mirror. It is interesting to note the difficulty some pupils have in displaying a range of facial expressions.

Gesture

Gesture can be intentional (adding emphasis to language) or unintentional ('leaking' an emotional state). Gestures include such movements as head nods/shakes, pointing, fist-making, folding of arms across the body, and rubbing of hands. If gestures do not match what is being said, they give out mixed messages that may cause confusion. They are subject to cultural variation so have the potential to be misinterpreted across cultures. As with facial expression, excessive gesturing may be distracting while lack of gesture may seem unresponsive.

Using picture cards or video clips of various gestures, ask the pupil to guess what the person is trying to communicate. Examples of possible gestures are:

- Wagging the forefinger (reprimand)
- Waving the hand in different ways, e.g. as a farewell greeting, or beckoning another to come
- Thumbs up (good/well done)
- Tip of forefinger and thumb touching, with other fingers together and up (OK)
- A pat on the back (congratulation)
- Hand in the air, palm facing forward (stop)
- Pointing with the forefinger (look)
- Forefinger to lip (be quiet)
- Arms held out a distance apart, palms facing inwards (size)
- Arm in the air, hand horizontal with palm down (height)
- Arm raised (seeking permission to speak or volunteering).

Alternatively, this activity could be done in a group as a game of charades.

Posture

There are two main postural positions – tension and relaxation. A very tense posture may convey anxiety and apprehension (sitting on the edge of a chair or a stiff upright posture); it may communicate lack of confidence and could make others uncomfortable or nervous. Equally, it could convey excitement, depending upon contextual cues. A listless posture (slouching, head bowed) may convey disinterest and apathy. It can be discouraging to another person in an interaction. In lessons, teachers may be irritated by this kind of posture in pupils, telling them to sit up and pay attention.

Using photos of people in different postures, ask the pupil what they think the person in the picture is feeling. Or, as a group activity, ask pupils in turn to mime different feelings indicated on cards by using posture only. To avoid facial cues, a neutral mask could be worn.

If working individually with a pupil who consistently adopts inappropriate postures, reverse role play could be used. The pupil plays the teacher and the adult plays the child, using the same postures the pupil often shows, e.g. slouching over the desk, head in hands, while being spoken to. Ask the pupil how they felt in the role of the teacher. This kind of role play should only be attempted when the pupil has established a trusting relationship with the adult concerned, so that the pupil does not perceive the teacher as putting them down.

Proximity

The use of personal space acts as a buffer zone in social situations, defining a person's territory. The context of the relationship and social situation defines what is a comfortable distance between people. Strangers will tolerate decreased personal space at a football match or on a crowded train. Sharing intimate space (less than 18 inches) other than in a queue or crowd, involves trust and a willingness to be intimate. A personal distance of half a metre to a metre is the usual distance for everyday social encounters and casual conversations. For more impersonal encounters such as in a shop, the distance is more likely to be in the range of one to three metres. When addressing a larger group of people, such as a class of children or in a performance, the distance will usually be greater still. Invading another person's personal space may be experienced as being pushy or 'in their face', creating discomfort for the other person. There are some children who alienate others at school by regularly invading their personal space.

This group activity requires adequate space, a large die, a spinner with sections marked forward or backward, and a set of instruction cards such as:

- Whisper your address to the person on your left

- Shake hands with the person on your right

- Shout 'Hello, would you like to come and play?' to the person opposite you

- Hold hands with the person on your left

- In a quiet voice, tell the person opposite you who lives in your house

- Ask the person two places to the right what their favourite colour is

- Speak in a loud voice to the whole group about your favourite pastime.

Take turns to throw the die and spin the spinner. Everyone in the group moves forward or backward the number of paces indicated by the fall of the die and the rotation of the spinner. Take turns to draw a card from the pack and carry out the instruction. The group then decides whether the distance between the people involved was well matched to the instruction. If not, what sort of distance would have been better?

Touch

Neutral body contact occurs within professional relationships (such as between a doctor and the patient they are examining) and in more formal social relationships (such as shaking hands when introduced to a stranger). Active body contact occurs within more personal and intimate relationships, such as parent to child or between close friends. It conveys affection or concern and indicates shared trust. We may see older children still using touch that would be more appropriately displayed by a younger pupil, for example a child at end of primary phase education still wanting to hug staff or classmates. They need to be helped to learn more appropriate interaction skills.

This activity could be completed as a discussion, but group role play is an alternative. A set of scenario cards needs to be created depicting a variety of situations, for example:

A classmate has fallen over and hit her head on a playground bench. She has a deep cut to her head which is pouring blood. A teacher is talking nearby and hasn't seen the incident. Do you:

a) stand quietly beside him until he notices you?

b) tap him gently on the arm and say excuse me please?

c) shake him roughly by the arm?

A group of children are playing a card game. You are keen to join in. Do you:

a) push one of them out of the way and squeeze in?

b) grab the nearest arm and tug hard, saying you want to play?

c) put your hand on someone's shoulder and ask if you can play?

You are introduced to a stranger. Do you:

a) nod and say hello?

b) give her a 'high five'?

c) fling your arms around her and give her a hug?

Listening

The activities suggested for eye contact are also appropriate when focusing on good listening skills. Circle Time activities provide a structure in which good listening skills may be developed. In schools, this involves children sitting in a circle and talking in turn on a given theme, often passing an object from child to child to indicate whose turn it is to speak. Additionally, there are games that can be played to develop good attention when listening, such as 'I went shopping and I bought ...' with each person adding an item in turn. Young children enjoy hearing favourite stories or rhymes with deliberate errors for them to detect. In a group, the children can compete for points, or in individual work, the child earns a point for each error spotted and the adult earns a point for each error missed.

Use of puppets

As discussed in chapter 5 on managing anger, working through puppets can be a useful way of making the learning less intrusive in sensitive situations because it removes the focus from the pupil. It can be used as an alternative to role play and is particularly useful in helping a pupil to develop empathy. In social skills work with younger children, puppet play can help them internalise socially appropriate ways of behaving. A key stage one child may enjoy taking a 'naughty puppet' home in a small suitcase with a sticker chart. They can practise teaching the puppet how to meet the social or behavioural targets indicated on the chart. Similarly, a shy puppet may be taught to become a little bolder. Therapeutic stories, discussed in the chapter 7, could be created around a puppet character.

Puppets can also be successfully used with older pupils by giving them the task to create a play to teach a particular skill to a younger audience.

Social skills groups

Group work lends itself well as a medium for developing social skills. There are some children who may need individual input first before being ready to cope in a social skills group, but a small group provides a helpful context in which to practise new skills. A group of six children is a good number to work with. If one or two are absent there remains a meaningful number to still be a group. When the number increases beyond six it becomes more difficult to keep every child engaged. Care needs to be taken in selecting children for group work to ensure a combination that is likely to work well. Such groups work well if they comprise children with differing areas of challenge. One impulsive, hyperactive child is usually plenty for any group! More would tend to increase the likelihood of them competing for attention. Nevertheless, such a child provides a good role model for the shy, withdrawn individual who is reluctant to talk, while the more introverted child becomes a useful role model in waiting and taking turns. Again, a group will function better with no more than one highly reserved child, as peers will find it difficult to wait long enough to give space to more reluctant contributors. Between these two extremes there will be others with more moderate challenges. The curriculum can be based on some of the skill areas discussed above, tailored to the specific needs of those taking part. The content needs to be different from class work, based largely around experiential activities and games. There are many great social skills games and activities available through educational suppliers. Games are an engaging way of building relationships and developing skills such as turn-taking and listening to one another. Further guidance on managing groups, including group rules and responding to unhelpful behaviour, is given in chapter 6 on 'Friendship skills'.

Lego® therapy

Lego therapy was pioneered by Dr Dan LeGoff, a clinical neuropsychologist in the USA. He noticed that autistic children who were disinterested in social interaction began socialising with each other when playing with Lego. He turned the collaborative building approach into Lego therapy, which has also been found to help children with social anxiety and language difficulties. Through Lego therapy, children can learn to communicate with others, express their feelings, develop problem-solving skills and change their behaviour. With adult support, the children work in pairs or triads. In a pair, the roles are:

- engineer/ supplier
- builder.

In a triad, the roles are:

- engineer (tells the supplier which pieces are needed and tells the builder how to put them together)
- supplier (finds the pieces described by the engineer and gives them to the builder)
- builder (receives pieces from the supplier and puts them together according to the instructions of the engineer).

It is the structure of this approach, with its clearly defined roles, that helps children who have difficulty socialising to develop communication and interaction skills. The roles can be supported by props such as builders' hard hats with labels stuck on, or badges on lanyards. The children take turns to try out the different roles, either within a session or in subsequent sessions. Some children may need individual pre-coaching to develop the necessary skills before beginning group work. As in all group work, some basic group rules are needed, such as:

- Structures must be built together by the group
- Keep to your own role
- Ask if you need help
- Use quiet indoor voices
- Speak kindly.

The adult's role is not to problem solve for the children but to notice if there is a problem and help the group to reflect upon what is happening. The adult helps the group to find ways to overcome the problem, then reflect on whether these have been successful. Sessions may require 45 minutes to an hour, depending on the complexity of the models and whether children swap roles within a session. Time needs to be allowed to play with the models once built. The children work from pre-designed plans but may, in time, go on to create their own designs.

Child-friendly principles of attunement

The wheel illustrated here was compiled by Gillian Shotton to illustrate some essential skills required for successful attunement/ interaction between two individuals. These could all be successfully explored during group work. Showing the young person video clips of seconds of interaction when they have demonstrated a skill from the wheel can be a very powerful way of helping them to repeat these behaviours.

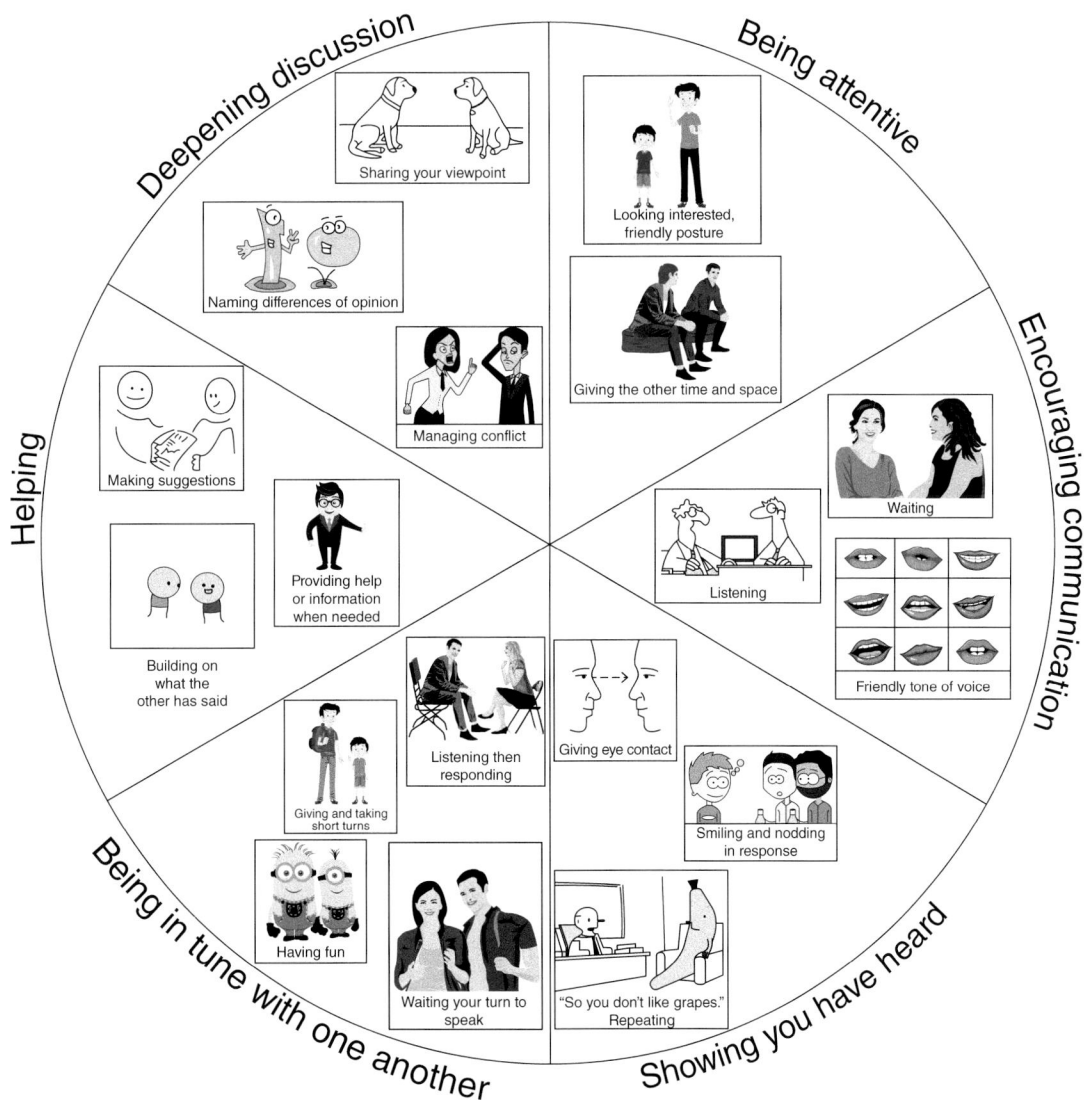

Deepening discussion

Sharing your viewpoint

Naming differences of opinion

Managing conflict

Being attentive

Looking interested, friendly posture

Giving the other time and space

Encouraging communication

Waiting

Listening

Friendly tone of voice

Helping

Making suggestions

Providing help or information when needed

Building on what the other has said

Listening then responding

Giving eye contact

Smiling and nodding in response

Giving and taking short turns

Having fun

Waiting your turn to speak

"So you don't like grapes." Repeating

Being in tune with one another

Showing you have heard

Social stories

Social stories can be a very effective approach to helping children and young people who have social or social communication difficulties to manage situations they find difficult. They were originally developed for those with autistic spectrum disorder who have difficulty understanding other people's perspectives, but they have also been found useful in supporting a wider range of needs. They are short stories, often just a paragraph or two, written in a specific style, to describe a chosen situation that the youngster finds challenging. This could, for example, be school assemblies, a subject lesson or perhaps a daily routine. They address issues that may be obvious to most people but not to those experiencing social difficulties.

The social story describes what people normally do in the specific situation, why they do it and common responses. The purpose of the story is to reduce anxiety and replace unhelpful behaviours with more appropriate ones. Rather than simply being directive, the story is designed to teach social understanding. Social stories are appropriate at all ages provided the language and presentation are matched to the youngster's understanding and level of maturity. They normally include drawings, pictures or photographs which add appeal and support understanding. They are ideally written in consultation with those who know the child well (such as class teacher or learning support assistant and parents) and after careful consideration of a specific challenge.

When writing a social story, it is important to target a specific situation or behaviour rather than trying to cover a range of different issues in one story. It needs to be tailored carefully to the child and should be based on a careful assessment of the situation. The story is written in the first person, and present or future tense (e.g. *Usually on a Friday afternoon we have a whole school assembly.*' Or, '*Next September I will go to a new school.*') They are short and to the point. Notice the way the following examples are written.

Changing schools

After the summer holidays, I will be going to Newtown Community School.

Newtown Community School is much bigger than the school I go to now and there will be lots more children there, many from other schools.

I feel a bit scared about this, but it helps me to think that my friends Hannah and Becky will also be going there, and we will be in the same form group.

Mrs Henderson will be our form tutor. We will go to her class for registration at the start of each morning.

After that we will walk to a different classroom for one of our lessons.

This will feel strange at first, but I will get used to it after a while.

I will have to look at my timetable to see which lesson I have next and which classroom to go to. I know that I will be with the rest of my class, so if I am not sure I will be able to follow them. If I get lost I know that I can always ask a teacher or another pupil to help me find my way.

I feel nervous about starting my new school but that's OK, because I know that most other children also feel a bit nervous about going. It's a big step and it's OK to feel a bit scared about all the changes. I will try to remind myself that new routines get easier with practice. I try my best in new situations.

Morning playtime

Each day at school there is a mid-morning break. All the classes stop work at the same time and usually the children go outside. Because there are lots of classes in our school, the cloakrooms and corridors are very busy with children getting their coats and snacks on the way to the playground. Most children like going out to play and they may be excited and noisy. Sometimes I find the noise too much and want to push others away. It is easier for me if I wait to the end of the queue.

In the playground, we sometimes play 'tag'. When you are 'it', you run after the other children in the game. You try to touch one of them and say, 'You're it', then it's their turn to chase. Sometimes the children scream with excitement when the one who is 'it' gets close to them. I like playing 'tag' with the others in my class. I will try not to be rough when I tag someone and just tap them gently on the arm or back. Then I can run away and wait to be chased. It is fun to play games with others. If someone tags me I will try to remember they are playing, not hurting me. I like to be kind to other children.

Social stories provide accurate information about real-life situations and, without relying on interpersonal contact, provide the young person with a prompt about how to respond. The young person is encouraged to read the story as often as is necessary to internalise the social messages. For this reason, the story should remain short and uncomplicated. Very young children would have the story read to them several times before entering the anxiety-provoking situation, and would be encouraged to follow the pictures.

In basic social stories, three different types of sentences are used (Gray 2015).

Descriptive sentences describe who does what, where this happens and why. For example:

My name is David. I go to Scouts in the village hall. Other boys from my school are also there. We play games and work towards badges. There are three helpers called …

Perspective sentences highlight how people feel from their perspective and how the child might feel. For example:

Most of the boys like to play indoor football. They enjoy chasing the ball around the hall, trying to score a goal against the opposite team. Sometimes I feel a bit scared when the ball comes near me.

Directive sentences describe the desired response to the target situation. For example:

I will try to join in.; Or 'I will try not to mind when I am tackled.

It is important to have a balance of these different types of sentence and the ratio is usually five or more descriptive and /or perspective sentences to one directive sentence.

To avoid over-literal interpretation, which is very important when working with children who have social communication difficulties, it is better to use words like *'usually'* or *'sometimes'*, otherwise the child may be dismayed when an exception arises. Similarly, the phrase *'I will try to …'* allows for the fact that it is hard to *always* get things right. Phrase like *'I can…'* or *'I will…'* are less flexible and appear to demand compliance. Social stories often end with a positive affirmation (e.g. *'I am a hard worker', 'I am a kind person'*) to help the child feel good about herself while learning new behaviours. Children who find social relationships challenging often experience reduced self-esteem.

The pupil reads or listens to the social story before the target situation arises. This may need to be daily (e.g. before playtime or assembly) and should continue for as long as the pupil wants or needs this support. Once the targeted behaviour becomes part of the child's repertoire, the story is no longer needed. It is however, useful to keep and revisit stories should a difficulty recur.

For more information on writing and using social stories, there is a useful book entitled *'Writing and Developing Social Stories'* by Caroline Smith (2016).

Case study

A group of year eight girls were highlighted as being a concern in school as they were continually getting into trouble in lessons and being sent out. Usually this was through them being cheeky and truculent with the teachers. The special educational needs co-ordinator (SENCO) outlined how she felt – that in many situations they were not deliberately being as surly as they might appear to be by the teachers. They did themselves no favours by speaking in a particular tone of voice or giving the teachers challenging looks, rolling their eyes etc. The SENCO thought that they often simply did not realise just how they were coming across and how they were alienating themselves from the teachers through their body language and tone of voice. Through a series of social skills sessions where video and role play was used extensively, the girls became more aware of how they were coming across through their verbal and non-verbal communication. They became more skilled at speaking in an appropriate tone of voice to staff as well as becoming more aware of their non-verbal communication. Watching themselves on the video often made them laugh as they had no idea of how they were coming across until they saw themselves in action. The opportunity to step back and be able to view their behaviour on film gave them an awareness of how others might perceive them as being hostile and challenging. This new awareness helped motivate them to change some of their habitual ways of responding in class so that they got into less trouble with the teaching staff. The girls started to learn how to employ techniques that would enable them to be better liked in school.

Summary

We have an inbuilt need to relate to others, and acquiring good social skills is essential to developing and maintaining successful relationships. These skills are primarily learned by watching others and much of our social behaviour develops within the family. Considerable socialisation also takes place in the context of school, and social skills development is a legitimate part of the curriculum. In this chapter, some important basic skills have been discussed. Ways of increasing pupils' social awareness have been considered, with many practical ideas suggested to promote experiential learning about basic skills. Children with social communication difficulties often find it hard to understand other children's feelings and behaviour. Social stories are a well-established approach to develop their understanding and promote pro-social behaviour. Some explanation and examples have been given to help those working with socially-challenged children to create bespoke stories fitted to tricky situations.

9. Supporting children through loss and bereavement

Introduction

Loss is an inevitable part of life. Children gain considerable experience of coping with loss through many common events like losing or breaking a treasured possession, a favoured activity becoming unavailable to them, friends moving away, a change of teachers, death of a pet and other such things. Even happy events can involve an element of loss. The arrival of a new baby in the family, for example, is likely to lead to reduced attention and perhaps the need to share a bedroom and belongings. If children learn to handle these changes with optimism, recognising that many other good experiences still lie ahead of them, they develop resilience to cope with life's losses.

Those losses mentioned above may be relatively small and common, but many children and young people find themselves facing change of a much greater magnitude. A sudden catastrophic accident or illness can lead to lifelong physical or learning disability that limits life opportunities. It is estimated that 200,000 children across England and Wales are affected by parental imprisonment, according to the Barnado's website in July 2017.

Children with a parent in prison are twice as likely to experience behavioural and mental health problems and do less well at school. They are three times more likely to be involved in offending behaviour themselves. Sixty-five per cent of boys with a convicted father will go on to offend themselves. Children with a parent in prison feel isolated and ashamed – unable to talk about their situation because of fear of being bullied and judged. The Barnado's website also reported that there are over 83,000 children in the care system in the UK. These children will have experienced significant losses which might include:

- loss of parents and extended family

- drop or break in contact

- loss of home, community

- loss of teams or clubs

- loss of familiar routine

- loss of items that hold important memories

- loss of privacy and choice

- loss of love and intimacy.

It is well established that children in care are more likely to have poor educational experiences, leave school with fewer qualifications, are at higher risk of offending, becoming a teenage parent and being not in education, employment or training. Many of the difficult behaviours that are seen in children in care could be in part due to an unresolved grieving process. Too frequently these children are viewed as disturbed rather than grieving (Fahlberg 1991).

Families are less stable units than they once were. Many children in school will experience family turbulence as parental marriages and partnerships are dissolved and new relationships formed. A report by Harry Benson in December 2010, carried out jointly by the Bristol Community Family Trust and the Centre for Social Justice, gave the figure of 48 per cent of couples with children breaking up before the first child reached the age of 16. Divorce was said to account for 20 per cent of break-ups, with unmarried families accounting for 80 per cent of break-ups. A significant proportion of children in the school population now live in single parent or reconstituted families. Most children of separating parents go through a period of unhappiness. Many experience a lowering of self-esteem, an adverse behavioural reaction and loss of contact with part of the extended family. Even those who have never known a father can experience an acute sense of loss and feel they are somehow different from their friends.

The loss that people are most keenly aware of, however, is the loss of a loved one through death. Whether it is sudden or predicted, the finality of the separation is a stark reminder of our mortality, often invoking the deepest questions that are the most difficult for anyone to answer. Many children will experience the death of a grandparent, some will be bereaved of a parent, and a few will lose a sibling or close friend. Over 24,000 children are bereaved of a parent each year in Britain, according to the website of the child bereavement charity Winston's Wish, with 4 per cent of children having experienced the death of a parent or sibling. In a study by Harrison and Harrington (2001) of over 1,700 secondary school pupils from two schools in northern England, 77 per cent aged 11 to 16 reported the loss of a close or significant relationship through death before the age of 16. This figure included friends as well as family members. A report by Wolfe et al (2014) published by the Royal College of Paediatrics and Child Health and National Children's Bureau, reported that over 3,000 babies died before the age of 1 year old and 2,000 children died aged between 1 and 19 years in the year 2012. Most schools are therefore likely to be confronted at some time by the need to support children who are directly affected by the death of another child. The death of a much-loved family pet can also be a hard-hitting loss for some children.

Whether the serious loss faced by a young person is a living loss or a loss through death, the process of grieving will have many similarities. Whatever the loss, it will be borne more easily if the child experiences sensitivity, support and understanding through the grieving process. Some will experience this adequately within their own family. For others, the parents' own grief may inhibit their ability to simultaneously recognise and meet their youngster's needs. It is a false assumption, however, that traumatic loss always leads to a need for counselling, though school staff often imagine this to be the case. Most bereaved children recover from their loss without the support of formal counselling. What they need most of all is the support of familiar and trusted adults. The most painful scenario is for their loss to be met with silence through fear of upsetting them.

The scope of this chapter is to assist understanding of the grieving process and suggest ways of supporting grieving children and young people within school.

The process of grieving

This used to be thought of as a linear process, with the bereaved person passing through stages of grief in a progressive way:

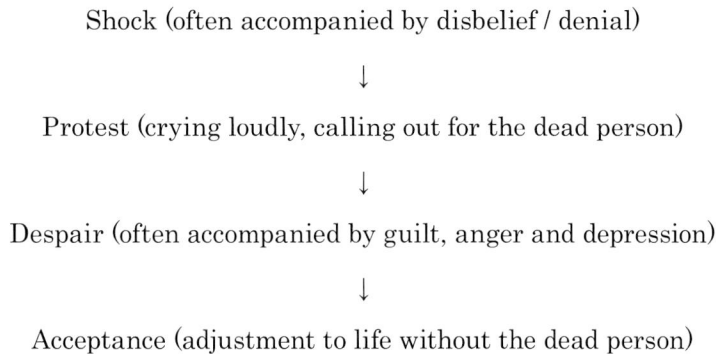

Shock (often accompanied by disbelief / denial)

↓

Protest (crying loudly, calling out for the dead person)

↓

Despair (often accompanied by guilt, anger and depression)

↓

Acceptance (adjustment to life without the dead person)

The grieving process is often thought to take up to two years, the first year (with its significant dates like birthdays and anniversaries) perhaps being the most traumatic. Inevitably the path will not be smooth, and grief can reappear with the triggering of special memories or connections with the dead person.

Perhaps a more useful model of the grieving process is the 'upward spiral of grief' suggested by Shelley Gilbert (2004). This model looks at grief as a journey from an initial emotional black hole, through an array of recurring feelings which become less intense with the passage of time. Those feelings include shock, disbelief, denial, sadness, anger, guilt, fear – though not in any prescribed order. There may also be some sense of relief, particularly where there has been an awareness of suffering. Such a mixture of emotions can feel enormously confusing, and the bereaved child may fear they are going mad. It is vital for them to have someone validate their confused emotions, letting them know it is normal for people to feel this way when someone they have loved has died. And all these feelings may be punctuated by moments of happiness and laughter. Times of feeling happy provide important opportunities for recuperation from the intensity of grieving. Rather than reaching a stage of acceptance, Gilbert suggests that adjustment is a more realistic description. The bereaved learn to live with the loss, acknowledging that life will never be the same again.

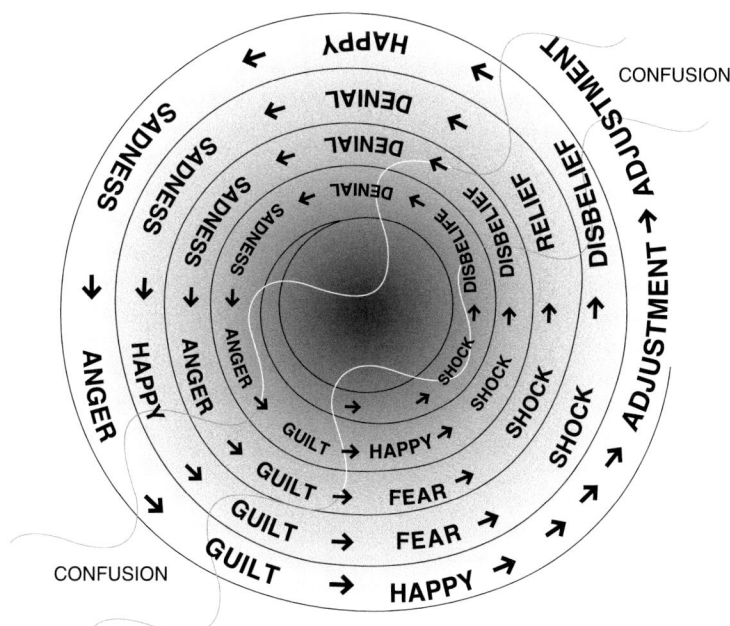

Upward Spiral of Grief (based on Gilbert, 2004)

Another model of grief that has been taught by Dr Lois Tonkin (1996) is that of growing around grief. This model challenges the idea that grief heals or diminishes over time. Instead the grief remains but a person's life adjusts over time to accommodate the pain of living with grief. Initially the loss is overwhelming and dominates all of life. It may be difficult to eat or sleep and hard to think about anything else. Rather than moving on from grief, the person grows around it. Over the ensuing months and years, new experiences in life and meeting new people all help to promote growth beyond the grief. The grief will probably always be there, and may even grow a bit bigger at difficult times, but it no longer completely dominates life. For many bereaved people, the idea of moving on or forgetting is one of the most problematic parts of grieving. Tonkin's model suggests that it is alright for grief to always be part of your life. The perspective changes over time so that it becomes more manageable to live with. Barbara Monroe (Monroe and Kraus 2009) used an analogy of a ball in a jar to refer to Tonkin's model. The jar represents life getting bigger while the grief remains the same size. The ball in the small jar represents grief initially, taking up most of the available space. In the biggest jar, the ball can roll around freely, leaving space for many other things. As the bereaved child's life expands the grief remains constant but their attention is taken up by many new experiences as well.

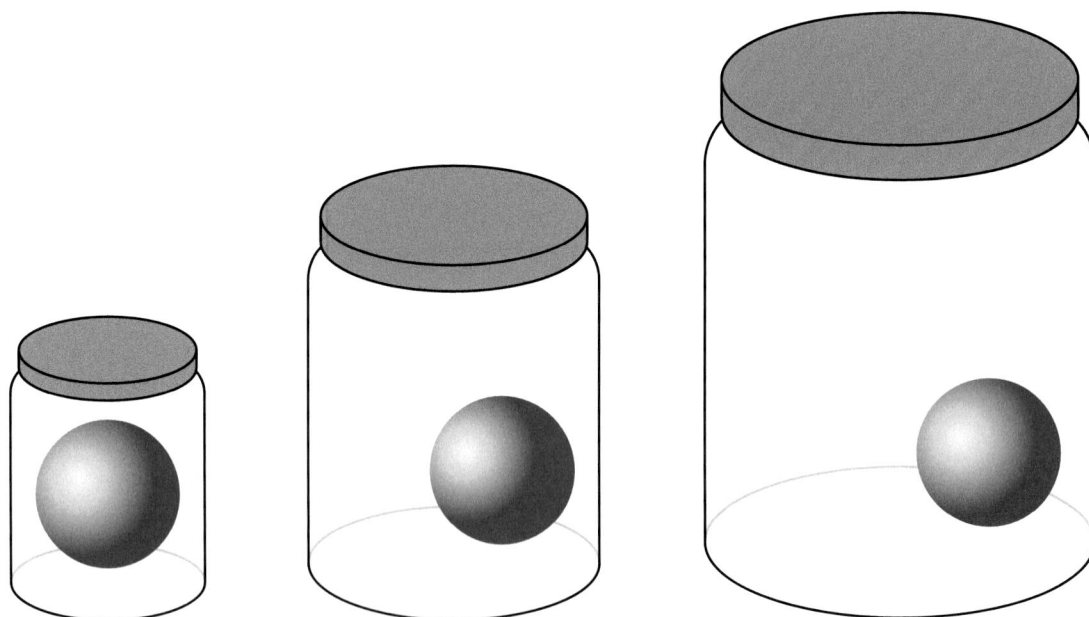

There are other models too, that represent the grieving process. It is important to remember that everyone is different, and each bereavement may affect people differently. A model simply aims to provide some understanding of a complex emotional adjustment and reinforces its normality within life.

Developmental responses to death

Cognitive development is strongly influenced by language skills. Limitations in language skills influence understanding of the situation and the child's expression of thoughts and feelings. Explanations of death need, therefore, to be matched to the developmental thinking and language skills of the child. Apply the Goldilocks principle, telling the child what they want to know, not too much and not too little.

In considering how to support children in school through the grieving process, it is important to take account of their level of intellectual and emotional maturity. The limited conceptual understanding of young children under the age of about 7 makes it difficult for them to appreciate the permanence of loss and death, and they may expect the dead person to return to them. When told about the death they might respond quite casually at the time, but start asking about death quite some time later. They tend to be very egocentric and somewhat magical in their thinking, seeing themselves as the centre of the universe. They see a causal link between their own thoughts, wishes and actions and what happens to themselves and other people. The small child may think that if they are always good, endure bad things and wait for a long time, the one they have lost will return to them. Others may come to fear any separation from their loved ones in case they lose them too, or even become fearful that they themselves might die. Young children use play to help them make sense of the world. While this may be distressing for the adults, it should be considered normal and healthy if the child is found re-enacting the cause of death or rituals surrounding it, such as the funeral.

Older primary age children begin to recognise the permanence of death, and understand that they themselves will one day die. Nevertheless, they are still somewhat concrete in their thinking and may be misled by the euphemisms adults often use to avoid talking directly of death. Hearing that 'We lost your granny', 'Mummy has gone to sleep', 'Grandpa is at rest now', or 'Your brother has passed away' can be confusing and ambiguous to say the least. Usually by around the age of 11 children can understand the finality of death in an adult way.

Young children are likely to ask very direct questions that may sound callous to adults. They are likely to ask about what happens to the body in the grave, or how the body gets burned at the crematorium. It is important to answer such questions honestly and as factually as possible, while being sensitive to judge how much the child really wants to know. But the most difficult questions to answer will be the ones that concern spiritual beliefs like, 'Where is Daddy now?' Adults in school need to respect the family's beliefs. It is important to be genuine and acknowledge difference by prefacing answers with phrases like, 'Some people believe ...' It is alright for supporting adults to admit that they do not have an answer to questions like, 'Where is heaven?' since uncertainty is an inescapable facet of our lives.

Often a young person will prefer to talk to a known adult than to a stranger. It is recommended that such support is made available flexibly, when the young person wants to talk. But it may also be helpful to have a certain time each week when the child knows they can go and talk to the adult in a prearranged place. This should continue for as long as the child wants it. ELSAs are well placed to offer this kind of support. Supporting a bereaved youngster is emotionally demanding and therefore it is important for the adult to have their own support to avoid becoming overwhelmed by the child's grief. It is strongly advised that no recently bereaved adult undertake this work because it may become difficult to separate personal grief from that of the young person.

Bereaved children will express their feelings in different ways. Some may become withdrawn, some aggressive, others nervous or fearful, or indeed a mixture of all these. It is not uncommon for children and young people to have trouble in sleeping, which exacerbates what is already a tiring process. As is the case for adults, their attention span when grieving will be less. They will experience intrusive thoughts that distract them from their work, and their learning is likely to be affected. Sometimes they will appear to cope well for a time, and behavioural changes may not become apparent until sometime later. The danger is that school staff will assume, because of the time lapse, that the changes are nothing to do with the bereavement the child has experienced.

In whatever way it is done, it is important that children do have the opportunity to grieve. If they never mourn their loss, their personality development may be affected so that they respond to any kind of loss in maladaptive ways.

Death of a close relative

Before a bereaved child returns to school, it is desirable to have had some contact with the family to find out how they would like information around their loss to be managed. It is usually helpful to prepare the other children, letting them know what has happened, and helping them to understand how their returning schoolmate is likely to be feeling. Encourage simple expressions of sympathy but discourage inquisitive questioning.

When the child returns to school, it is helpful for them to receive acknowledgement of their loss and for appropriate pastoral support to be made available to them. While normal routines are reassuring, the young person may need to withdraw at times if they feel overwhelmed or tearful. Identifying a trusted adult to whom they may go for support at such times is reassuring, even if the support does not turn out to be needed.

Schools that employ an ELSA are well placed to offer a young person regular times and space to talk about their loss, should they want it. But not all youngsters will want to talk. Being allowed to be quiet can be equally helpful, especially if linked to a practical activity. One such activity that is often used is to make a memory box in which the child can keep some special items to remind them of the loved one they have lost. An excellent website has been created by the charity Winston's Wish to support children and young people who have lost relatives and close friends. Support materials can be downloaded for use by staff in schools. There are also areas on the website for children only, where they can post their memories, read of others' grief, complete activities and access a secure chat room for young people, monitored to ensure their protection.

Case studies

Harry, in year three, was living with his terminally ill mother. He has significant language and literacy difficulties, so was receiving support on a daily basis for his learning needs. This enabled him to talk to the learning support assistant regularly about anything that was worrying him. Because of his learning difficulties he found it hard to understand the seriousness of the situation, and thought his mother's hair loss rather funny. The family prepared him well for the changes ahead and he knew before his mother died that he would be going to live with his father, stepmother and her children. He had many preparatory visits and built up good relationships with his new family. The LSA often talked with him about moving to another home and how he felt about the changes. After the death of his mother Harry didn't remain long at the school, transferring instead to one nearer his new home. In the interim, however, he was able to talk to the LSA about his mum's death. He accepted the explanation his family had given him that Mum had gone to heaven. He was never tearful or really upset. The LSA thought being able to talk freely without any awkwardness had helped.

...

Eight-year-old Ben, usually a lively, cheerful boy, was becoming upset in class whenever things he was doing reminded him of Nan. She was in hospital, having been diagnosed with cancer. One time when he was tearful, the school ELSA was asked to talk with him. Ben was glad to talk about why he was upset. He told Mrs Morris that he didn't feel he could cry or talk about Nan's illness at home because Mum was so upset herself. He felt he had to keep his feelings to himself to protect her. Ben said that although he was younger than his brother, his mum talked more to him about Nan's illness because he didn't show how sad he felt. Ben said it was good to be able to talk to someone who wouldn't get upset. Mrs Morris told him it is natural to feel sad when someone you love is ill and that it's good to cry. They finished their time together by playing a game, and Ben returned to class knowing that he could talk to her whenever he needed. The next time he came to her he said Nan only had a short time to live, so they made a card for Ben to take to the hospital. It was the end of term but after the summer holidays Ben found Mrs Morris in the playground to tell her Nan had died. She asked if he would like to talk about it but he said he didn't need to. He was feeling better because Mum had stopped crying and he could talk to her now.

...

Kelly, age 7, was having upsetting dreams about Grandma who had died the year before. Mrs Wood talked with her about the dreams and Kelly said how much she missed her Grandma. Mrs Wood suggested they make a memory box, which Kelly was pleased to do. They spent three sessions making and decorating a box, thinking about what to put in it. Mum helped Kelly choose some photos and Kelly told Mrs Wood some things to write for the box. A few weeks later Kelly's mum came to tell Mrs Wood that Kelly was no longer having disturbing dreams.

...

Eleven-year-old Jack arrived in school very upset because Granddad had died the previous day. The ELSA was asked to see him. Jack, old enough to be very aware of the circumstances, told her in great detail what had happened, even though he found it very distressing. Mrs Reed was able to explain some of the medical terminology to him. Jack also wanted to know how he could help his dad feel better. They met again the next day. Jack wanted to do something at the funeral, so he and Mrs Reed looked through some poems which Jack took home to share with Dad. The day before the funeral Jack showed Mrs Reed the poem he had chosen to read at the service. A few days later they talked again about how he was feeling and how things were at home. The Christmas holidays arrived and when the new term started Mrs Reed checked up on Jack. He was feeling better and said he didn't think he needed any further help.

...

Eleanor was 13 when her father died. She didn't know him very well as her parents had separated – Mum had remarried and her father lived abroad. Eleanor grieved that she didn't know much about her father and had lost the opportunity to ever get to know him better. For a while the school ELSA met with her each week. They made a memory box for items that reminded her of her father. Eleanor covered it with shells and put inside a picture of a boat as he was fond of the sea. While they worked on this, Eleanor talked about her family and what she had been told about her father. She appreciated this time to reflect with someone who was able to listen to the thoughts she needed to express but couldn't say at home.

Death in a school

When a pupil or member of school staff dies, the impact is on a larger scale than the personal loss referred to above. In this case greater numbers of children will be affected, as well as the adults who work in the school. It is important for factually accurate information to be provided as quickly as possible to reduce the risk of inaccurate rumours spreading. It is usual to gather the most directly affected pupils together to deliver the sad news to them as a group, but also to disseminate the news in a co-ordinated way across the school, either in class groups or in a whole school assembly. The widespread use by pupils of social media will, however, make this more difficult as news tends to travel too fast for the school to manage. Even if the news is already spreading, it is wise to gather pupils together to share facts and discourage rumours.

Some flexibility in these circumstances needs to be shown with respect to normal school routines. Children and young people are unlikely to be able to receive the news and return immediately to work as if nothing has happened. They need to be allowed an opportunity to talk about the person who has died or the circumstances surrounding their death. It is also advisable to reduce the intellectual demands of the work the class goes on to do immediately afterwards as dealing with loss reduces people's capacity to concentrate. Those most directly affected are likely to need greater support, and the normal timetable may need to be suspended for these pupils to allow them to openly express their grief and concern.

It can often be helpful to allow children the opportunity to plan memorials for the child or teacher who has died. Classmates may wish to make a card for the bereaved family, write special memories of the person they have lost, including memorial poems, or draw pictures. Children may wish to participate in planning a longer-term memorial to the person who has died, such as the planting of a tree or making a memorial collage. It is important to encourage the children to express their feelings in these ways, while nevertheless encouraging a return to normal routines as soon as is reasonably possible. At times of bereavement, children will need increased opportunities to talk about how they feel. It will be normal for the new loss to bring up memories of previous losses in their lives, and these should be acknowledged. Some children will cope much more easily with the change that bereavement brings, but others may need special additional support, either individually or in a small group. It is not easy to predict which children will need additional support, since it is impossible to know what personal memory or worry might be triggered by a traumatic event. It is important therefore not to be too quick to dismiss any child's response as exaggerated or attention-seeking without listening to them.

While educational psychologists are often called upon to support schools through sad or traumatic events, it is widely recognised that it is usually the adults most familiar to the children who are in the best position to offer direct support initially. An important function of those staff is to help children know that their reactions are normal and to be expected. It is helpful to share with the children, in a way that is appropriate to their age and development, some of the characteristics of grief to help them make sense of the conflicting thoughts and emotions they will experience. A few children may go on to need more specialised help from external agencies if they continue to be troubled over a longer period than their peers, or if there are complicating factors in their bereavement.

Case study

An 11-year-old boy was killed while crossing the road. Some of his friends were given support at the time, but teachers hadn't realised that David had been a friend and neighbour of the boy since they were both little. It was eight months later that David was referred to the ELSA because he was having a lot of time off school. David admitted that he sometimes went to call for his friend before remembering that he was no longer there. Mrs Ewing showed him the spiral of grief (from the Grief Encounter resource pack), explaining the normality of his feelings. She listened as he talked about the times they had spent together as friends. It was easier for David to do this with an ELSA than his family, who had also been affected by the tragedy. They met regularly for several months and also worked on anger management, as he was sometimes disruptive in class. David responded well to individual work and has sometimes asked to see Mrs Ewing again to talk through problems. She talks with his head of year to help resolve some issues for him.

Complex grief

Any bereavement involving suicide, murder or accidental death may produce a more complex grieving process than death by natural causes. If the bereaved directly witnesses the death, post-trauma symptoms may well occur. This is not to say that everyone involved in a traumatic bereavement will require a high level of support. Their personal resilience factors will moderate their response.

Indicators of post-traumatic response could include re-experiencing of the event, either through intense flashbacks or intrusive thoughts and images that cause the event to be re-lived. There could also be avoidance responses such as numbing of feelings, refusal to think about the incident or people associated with it, a sense of distance from family and friends, and feelings of hopelessness about the future. Heightened arousal can also occur, shown by difficulty sleeping, irritability and volatility, possible aggression, inability to concentrate and hyper-vigilance.

Children who experience grief of this kind are more likely to need additional professional support from specialist agencies. Such support is not usually accessed immediately, as initially they are unlikely to be ready to process what has happened.

Family break-up

Family breakdown will usually be preceded by stress within the family. Often this will include disharmony between parents, between a parent and one or more of the children, or acute relationship difficulties between siblings. Having a child with serious developmental difficulties is known to be a risk factor for family breakdown. Other risk factors include family poverty, parental mental health difficulties and parental alcohol or substance abuse.

Looking at the impact of family breakdown on children, a study by Dunn and Deater-Deckard (2001) identified some key factors that increased children's resilience through the changes:

- Low or suppressed conflict between parents

- Parents communicating well with each other

- Resident parent facilitating contact with absent parent

- Arrangements negotiated with the children

- Regular contact schedules established and maintained

- All parties committed to the contact

- Children encouraged to talk about their thoughts and feelings

- Minimised disruption to children's support networks – family, friends, school and extra-curricular activities.

Grandparents and friends were found to be the key confidants in the period immediately following separation. Children who were close to their maternal grandparents were found to have fewer adjustment problems. No explanation was offered for this, but one might wonder whether contact with maternal grandparents may be greater following separation because more children remain with their mothers than with their fathers. Maternal grandparents may often provide more support, therefore, to the single mother with childcare. Confiding in fathers and siblings was found to be rare. Confiding and emotional closeness were found to be less common with step-parents rather than birth parents. This was also apparent with parents who had experienced more adversity in their lives, such as teenage pregnancies or several changes in relationship.

Dunn and Deater-Deckard's study revealed that most children had very little communication with their parents about family change. Very few indeed were given any explanation of what had happened to bring about the breakdown in relationship between the parents or what would happen as a result. Twenty-five per cent of the children said that no one had talked to them about the separation when it happened. Only 5 per cent had been given full explanations and been able to ask questions. Most children reported having been confused and distressed. Children who had difficult, negative relationships with either father or mother were more likely to be anxious, depressed, worried, aggressive or have problems at school. It was not clear whether the poor relationship caused the adjustment problems or vice versa. Children who experienced their fathers or stepfathers as not emotionally close were almost three times more likely to be reported by teachers as having problems at school.

Many children said they missed their non-resident parent very much indeed and longed to see more of them. They made practical suggestions on how to achieve this. One child commented that he would like to see his father at weekends rather than on weekdays, because they did not get time to talk on schooldays. Others said they wanted to do things with their non-resident parents, not simply watch television. The unreliability of non-resident fathers was a common theme and caused much distress.

Importantly, the children who said they had been consulted about living arrangements were more likely to report positive feelings about the two-household life. Fifty per cent were positive about dividing their lives between two homes. This was helped by having an active role in the arrangement and being able to talk to their parents about the challenges associated with divided lives. Children were very sensitive to criticism of one parent by the other and to conflict between birth parents. The presence of criticism would inhibit their inclination to talk freely to parents.

Most children will show some changes in school behaviour following parental separation. There will often be deterioration in work standards, accompanied by inattentiveness, restlessness, and increased daydreaming, but only some will openly express their sadness. Younger children will frequently blame themselves, genuinely believing that they are the cause of their parents' problems. 'If only I had been good, daddy would have stayed,' is often an unspoken but underlying belief. Sometimes adolescents too can feel that they are at the root of their parents' disagreements. The authors have also known cases where adolescents seem to have chosen disruptive and challenging behaviour as an attempt to re-engage a separated parent in their life.

When faced with considerable emotional stress, some children may revert to behaviours more characteristic of an earlier stage of social and emotional development. Others may not actually regress, but may fail to move on and mature in the same way as their peers. Their friendships can potentially become vulnerable, leading to even greater loss, and they may need support in developing or maintaining social relationships with peers.

The familiarity of school routines can of itself provide some comfort for the distress of a disrupted home life. Yet there may be times when the young person needs some space to talk about the anxieties the changes bring. School may be the only place where they can find a neutral adult who will listen and not judge. The emphasis will need to be on listening rather than advising, since every child's experience is unique, and they will need to find their own ways of coping with the difficulties they face.

Children are more likely to come to terms with parental separation when they can recognise the loss as a breakdown in the relationship between their parents, not a rejection of themselves by the parent who has left the family home. This is much harder for a child to believe if the departing parent is inconsistent in maintaining contact with their child. Nevertheless, older youngsters may be helped to consider the conflicting pressures that their parents face and see that situations can be viewed from a variety of perspectives. This can be assisted by encouraging the young person to wonder how Dad might be feeling or thinking about some aspect of the family situation, how Mum might be feeling or thinking, the differing pressures on their respective parents, etc.

Because of the strong emotions evoked by family breakdown, it can sometimes be difficult for children and young people to talk about their feelings to their parents. It may at times be appropriate for a member of staff in whom the youngster has confided, to seek the youngster's permission to share their feelings or anxieties with their parents. If the child wishes to write or send a picture to the absent parent, this too could be supported by a trusted member of staff. This should be with the knowledge and permission of the parent with whom the child is living, unless the young person is old enough to be judged competent to make such decisions on their own. This would normally apply to older adolescents.

A further source of tension for children is the arrival of a step-parent. No matter how well liked the adult may be, children will usually at some point protest, 'You're not my Dad!' (or Mum). This is especially likely when they cannot get their own way. Sometimes the child will work very hard to undermine the new relationship. A supportive adult in school can provide an outlet where feelings of anger or resentment may be worked through. Then, if the youngster is sufficiently mature, they may be helped to understand how it might be for the step-parent who has taken on some care and responsibility for a child who is not their own.

Let's get practical

In supporting a bereaved child, it is important to be led by their readiness to talk. Sometimes they may seem to be reluctant to talk about what has happened. It helps to have an activity upon which to focus. An activity that has often been found to engage a child well is the making of a memory box. This involves decorating a special box and putting into it special reminders of the loved one who has gone. This may include photos and small treasured possessions. It may also include short written accounts of special things the child and loved one did together and drawings or poems in memory of them. It could include a letter written to the loved one where the child is able to say how they feel about them and express gratitude for shared times. This is a gentle way of acknowledging the experiences no longer available while recognising, nevertheless, that good memories can live forever with those who remain. The making and filling of the box allows for times of natural conversation and times of silent contemplation. It then leaves the child with a tangible reminder of their loved one that they can pick up, look through and maybe add to, whenever they need, in private moments of remembrance.

A member of school staff may be asked to work with a child to prepare them for impending bereavement, for example the death of a terminally ill parent. In a similar way, a special treasure box may be created to store mementos, photos and happy memories. The sick parent may wish to contribute their own messages and memories of special times to leave with their son or daughter. In this scenario, close liaison with the family is vital to ensure the member of staff is aware of what others are telling the child. This enables the supporting adult to answer questions in a way that is sensitive to family wishes.

For younger children, there are story books available with which they may identify. The storyline is intended to be therapeutic, exploring issues that are likely to concern the child while helping them to know how other children face similar sadness of their own. These can be a useful starting place for support work with a child. Most young children enjoy sharing a book with an adult. If not ready to talk about their own circumstances directly, they may be encouraged to think and talk about the characters in the story. Non-fiction books too, may be available for older readers, addressing the practicalities of life in a separated family. It is helpful to have a variety of books available in a school library so that children and young people can also choose to access them with relative privacy. School library services are a useful source of advice about books that are available for different age groups.

Marge Eaton Heegaard has written several books and workbooks that relate to loss, bereavement and change, some titles being:

- *When Someone Very Special Dies*
- *When Someone Has a Very Serious Illness*
- *When Mom and Dad Separate*
- *When a Family is in Trouble*
- *Grief: A Natural Reaction to Loss*
- *Living Well with My Serious Illness*
- *Beyond the Rainbow: A Workbook for Children in the Advanced Stages of a Very Serious Illness*

These, and others by the same author, can be worked through with a child to trigger discussions about their own experiences.

When a child in school dies, it is helpful for staff members to include friends and classmates in decision making about memorials. Creating a special garden or planting a tree together provide natural opportunities for children to talk about their loss, and even about their own fears arising from their friend's premature death. Releasing helium balloons with personal messages attached can be a comforting way of saying goodbye.

A child whose parents have separated may need individual time with a supporting adult in school to process the feelings this change has brought to their life. Sometimes group work in school, bringing together children who have experienced parental separation, has been a successful support approach. Key aims might be to:

- acknowledge and normalise diverse family situations and to discuss some of the difficulties inherent in them

- help children name, understand and normalise their feelings about their new family structure and the family structure they have lost

- recognise positive as well as negative aspects of their families

- focus on a positive future, accepting those things they can and cannot have control over

- promote peer support.

Looking after yourself

Teaching and support staff in school need always to be aware of the limits of their own competence in dealing with the emotional needs of the children in their care. It is no failure to recognise when a child's distress is too great or complex for them to adequately support, and referral to other agencies is desirable.

There are some key points worth noting by those who may be called upon to support grieving youngsters in school. Those who are grieving themselves should be wary of trying to actively support others while still trying to come to terms with their own personal grief. It can become difficult for the adult to separate their own feelings from the feelings of the child and the adult themselves may become overwhelmed by the situation. It is perfectly appropriate to say, 'Not me, not at this time.'

Yet even when there has been adjustment to personal losses, the very nature of empathy will lead to some degree of personal impact from other people's grief. It is therefore very important that a supporting adult has someone with whom they can offload the strong emotions their involvement is likely to evoke. This type of sharing is commonly referred to as professional supervision. It is desirable that all staff in an emotional support role routinely have professional supervision arrangements, but even more important to ensure appropriate support when dealing with more emotive issues like loss and bereavement.

Summary

Coming to terms with loss is a normal part of life and something which children will experience at all kinds of levels. Many schoolchildren experience loss arising from breakdown of parental relationships and a significant number also experience bereavement of a close relative or friend. This chapter has explored the process of grieving, which has similarities whatever the nature of the loss. It has referred to some specific kinds of loss and bereavement that school staff may encounter when supporting children. It has attempted to demystify the kind of support that most grieving youngsters are likely to need from those who know them best, a key part of which is to help children and young people realise that their reactions to loss are normal and experienced by others too.

10. Resilience

Introduction

Resilience refers to your ability to adapt to stressful circumstances or crises. More resilient individuals are able to manage and adapt to difficult situations. Resilience has been described as, 'normal development under difficult conditions' (Fonagy et al 1994). It embodies the idea of being able to 'roll with the punches' and cope with the 'slings and arrows' that life throws at you, rising above adversity (Hill et al, 2007).

Theory and practice have often focused on the negative consequences of experiencing adverse circumstances. This is understandable as there is much evidence that shows how difficult early experiences and a lack of a secure attachment have an impact on brain development, emotional regulation and learning (e.g. Teicher and Sanson 2016). Nevertheless, some children do well despite difficult circumstances. Rather than focusing on what has gone wrong, a resilience approach looks at what we can learn from children and young people who, in the face of very difficult circumstances, have managed to cope well and rise above their adversity. A resilience-led perspective is optimistic and pragmatic; it views change as always being possible and looks to tap into and build upon strengths that a young person may have.

Factors underlying resilience

What makes some people more resilient than others? There are certainly wide variations in outcomes for individuals who go through very similar experiences. Many people believe their level of resilience is due to their personality, that perhaps they are too sensitive and so less resilient, or they see themselves as thick-skinned and so perhaps more resilient. Research shows that internal factors, such as personality, do play a role but they are not the whole story. Resilience is not a fixed trait that a person does or does not have. Whether you are resilient depends on a complex interaction between:

- The nature and amount of adversity experienced
- The timing/spacing between adverse events that have occurred
- External protective factors, e.g. the presence of a caring relationship, positive school experiences
- Internal protective factors, e.g. self-regulation skills, self-efficacy, optimism.

To illustrate this, Gillian Shotton has created the following model that summarises some of the key internal and external protective factors.

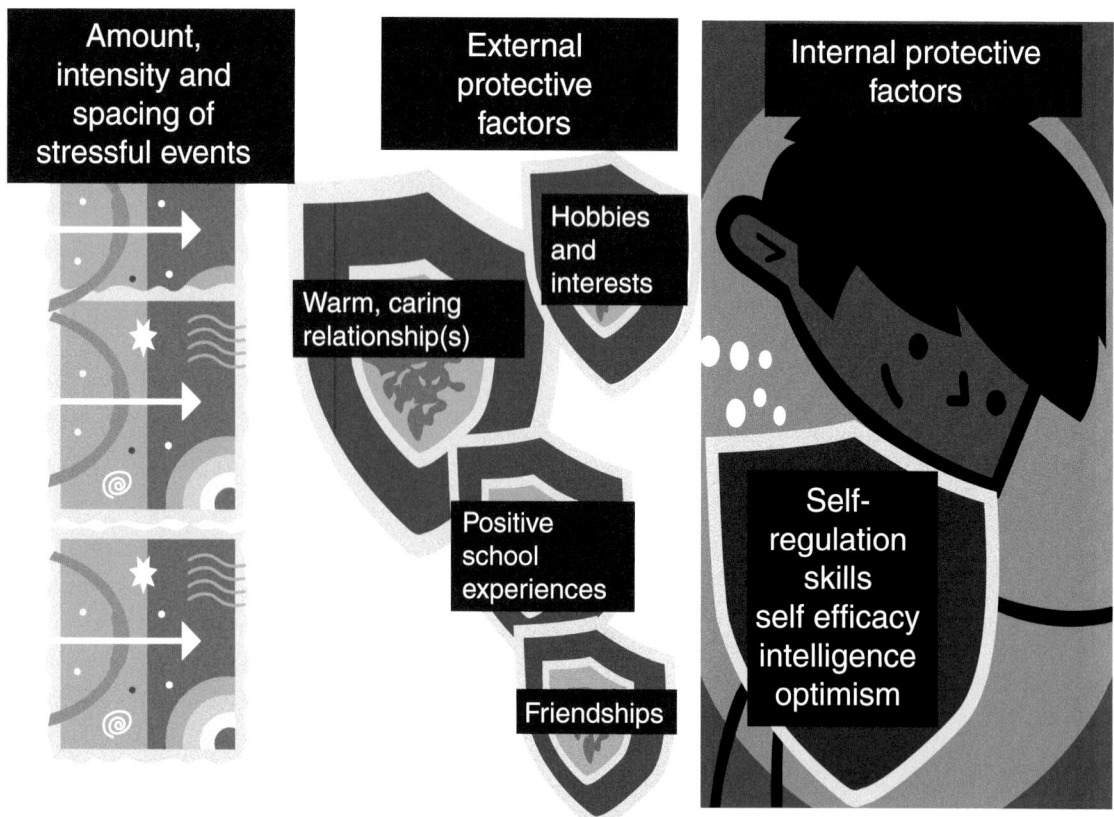

The nature and amount of adversity experienced

The arrows shown on the left represent the slings and arrows of life, the nature and quantity of adverse events we experience. Decreasing the stockpile of negative events is helpful as it can give the positive factors a better chance of having an impact and helping someone be resilient through difficult times (Gilligan 2001). Even if you can decrease the stockpile of adverse circumstances by just one, you can make a significant difference to a young person's life. For example, you are unlikely to be able to change home factors, such as a father's alcoholism, but perhaps in school another situation the young person finds difficult and stressful is eating in the busy dining hall. If you can remove this stressor from the young person's life by making alternative lunchtime arrangements a possibility, you may well have increased this young person's capacity for being resilient.

It is worth noting that there is often a negative spiral or chain of adverse events. One event, e.g. rejection from a parent, may then lead to another negative event, such as joining a peer group that demonstrates antisocial behaviour, leading to the person joining in with this behaviour and consequently getting into trouble with the police, and so on (Rutter 1999).

Risk factors

There are factors that are associated with low levels of resilience. These include the following:

- Family breakdown/parental conflict
- Domestic abuse
- Children from conflict zones
- Abuse, neglect
- Parental substance abuse
- Parents with physical or mental health needs that prevent the child's needs being met.

External protective factors

The shields in the centre of the model represent external protective factors. These are factors external to the individual that are associated with resilience. You will notice that the largest of these is the one entitled 'Warm, caring relationship(s)'.

The importance of the early attachment relationships between carer(s) and child is now well established. Advances in neuro-imaging technology have confirmed the link between having a warm, caring, attuned relationship and the development of the brain (e.g. Perry 2000; Teicher and Sanson 2016).

Working in a school situation you may be aware of a child or young person who has not experienced, and does not currently have, a warm caring relationship with their primary carer. It is important to recognise that even though this may be the case, other relationships can help to form a child's or young person's secure base. Your relationship with them, or a relationship they have with another member of staff in school, can be a critical external protective factor for their resilience. As we grow older, the relationships that constitute our secure base expand but we never lose the need for support, encouragement and consolation (Gilligan 2001). It is often our experience working in schools, that for some children and young people, a relationship with one or two key members of staff has been the most consistent and stable relationship in their lives. Research carried out by Baumeister (2005) showed that if a rejection experience was followed by an opportunity to make a new relationship, then individuals were keen to take that opportunity. A secure base (the presence of a warm, caring relationship) is described by Daniel and Wassell (2002) as underpinning all other dimensions of resilience.

For example, one young person, who had almost no opportunity to attend a mainstream school and an appalling range of adverse circumstances in her life, managed to achieve a good honours degree. The only identifiable protective factors were a love of reading and an English teacher who took a special interest in her (Jackson and Martin 1998).

Positive school experiences make it more likely that young people will then be able to organise their lives more effectively, making planned decisions about their careers and marriage (Quinton and Rutter 1988). The mechanism for this is uncertain but Rutter (1999) feels it is likely that success in one area enhances self-esteem and self-efficacy, making it more likely for individuals to feel more confident in handling new challenges. A study of women who had experienced sexual abuse when they were young found that positive school experiences helped to distinguish those who had done better in terms of their recovery (Romans et al 1995).

Developing proficient and fluent reading skills, along with a love of reading, has been found to be an important protective factor for helping young people who have been through very difficult circumstances to go on and live successful lives (Jackson and Martin 1998). Reading can also be a useful escape into another world, so can provide opportunities for relaxation and peace which might not otherwise happen. There is also evidence that reading fiction helps to develop empathy (Kidd and Castano 2013), another important skill in terms of emotional self-regulation.

Let's get practical

- Take an interest in the young person and find out about their hobbies and interests.

- Emotional literacy sessions, either one to one or in a group, are an excellent opportunity to get to know the young person better and develop a positive relationship with them.

- Giving the young person a position of responsibility in school is another way of communicating that you like and value them. It also helps them to see school in a more positive light if they are contributing to aspects of school life, rather than just being a receiver.

- Make books available for taking home and enjoying.

- Give input to parents/carers on enjoying and sharing books together, making books a part of their daily routine. Even for teenagers, finding ways to share books together, e.g. reading a chapter after a meal while everyone is still around the table, is beneficial.

- Put in place appropriate reading interventions to improve literacy but avoid making it aversive. Some phonics programmes can detract from enjoyment of reading and books through sheer boredom. Paired reading is an excellent evidence-based intervention that emphasises enjoying books together.

- As well as through education, there are also opportunities for warm, caring relationships through friendships and through hobbies and interests, both of which, you will see from the model, represent external protective factors (shields) in their own right. The aim then, is to make the most of the potential offered by anyone (extended family, sports coach, teachers, friends etc.) who takes an interest in the child or young person.

Hobbies and interests also give the young person an opportunity to develop talents through which they can then feel good about themselves. This can then make a huge contribution to their resilience. Maybe things are not going well at home or at school but if they feel they are getting better at football and make a positive contribution to the team, this can help them be more resilient. The difficulties are still there, but hobbies and sports represent a chance to escape from them for a while and may give rise to feelings of competence.

- Look at talents, skills and strengths with a young person. A great way to do this is to use strength cards, getting them to sort them into three piles – those they feel are just like them, those they feel are not like them and those they feel are sometimes like them.

- Find clubs they might be able to join that would develop their talents.

- Find out what they enjoy and direct them to hobbies or activities in the local area that they might be able to join in with.

- Provide opportunities in school for relevant clubs and activities; this might include going beyond the comfort zone of the staff to accommodate the special interests of the young people, e.g. Minecraft club or scooter club.

Friendships are another important factor in resilience. Knowing there is a small group of friends with whom you can talk and have some fun with when times are difficult, helps people to carry on in difficult times.

- Look at setting up a Circle of friends; see chapter 6 on friendship skills for more ideas on how to go about this.

- Provide opportunities for special project work in groups to foster friendships that you think will be positive for the young person.

- Encourage friendships by giving them special joint positions of responsibility.

Internal protective factors

Self-regulation skills, being able to manage your attention, emotions and subsequent behaviour, play a significant role in resilience levels. Research links such skills to good adaptation over a person's life (Carlson, White and Davis-Unger 2014; Masten 2014). Key to self-regulation is the area of executive function. Executive function is a range of thinking that takes place in the pre-frontal cortex. It includes being able to inhibit yourself doing something you feel like doing in favour of a better option, being able to plan, being able to reflect and being able to regulate your behaviour. Executive function skills seem to be a key factor in helping high risk children to be resilient in a context of severe adversity or poverty (Blair and Raver 2012).

Executive function skills are also associated with better school adjustment. In the famous marshmallow study, Mischel and colleagues (1972) found that children who were able to resist the temptation to eat a marshmallow now, in order to wait for a larger reward 15 minutes later, showed greater competence and had fewer problems in adolescence and early adulthood than those who were unable to resist. Something to bear in mind though, is that a follow-up study at the University of Rochester (Marshmallow Study Revisited, 2012) suggested that the ability to wait also depends on how much you trust the adult involved to come back with the goods! So, it stands to reason that children who have experienced adults being unreliable and, perhaps, have experienced neglectful or abusive parenting, will be less likely to be able to wait, as this has not been an adaptive strategy for them. They have greater doubts that the adult will be true to their word and return with two marshmallows.

Children who have a sense of self-efficacy have a belief that they can exercise control over their world and can change things; they believe that what they do will have an impact on outcomes for them. Self-efficacy beliefs develop from having frequent opportunities to have an impact on your environment, to gain a sense of control and agency, by being given manageable challenges where you can experience success. A strong sense of self-efficacy fosters persistence in the face of adversity. Self-efficacy beliefs are often specific to particular domains, so a person might feel a sense of self-efficacy with regard to maths but not with sticking to a diet!

Many studies of resilience have found there is an association between resilience and intelligence. There is evidence that having a level of intelligence that is average or above is a protective factor, particularly when adversity levels are high (Rutter 1999). Other longitudinal studies have also found intelligence to be a protective factor (e.g. Losel and Farrington 2012). To develop thinking skills and understanding requires an individual to be in an environment where there are opportunities for learning and development. Stress, illness, sleep deprivation, homelessness etc. would inhibit such opportunities for development. Intelligence can also be a double-edged sword, in that sometimes a lack of understanding can be protective (Masten 2014).

In many case studies and research studies, resilience is associated with optimism and believing that life has meaning. Classic works on resilience often outline that those who overcame immense adversity had a more positive, optimistic outlook on life (e.g. Frankl 1959).

Let's get practical

- Emotional literacy is a big part of self-regulation; being able to recognise and manage your emotions is a key skill for resilience. This book has a wealth of ideas and practical suggestions for developing those skills.

- If you can help a young person just to start talking about their worries and concerns by giving them time and space and forming a supportive relationship with them, then that in itself will have helped to increase their resilience. If you can work with them on finding appropriate ways of expressing those difficult emotions rather than acting on them in socially unacceptable ways, then you will have helped them to become more resilient.

- Teachers and caregivers can foster a sense of self-efficacy by providing opportunities for children and young people to experience their impact on the environment, giving them graduated steps with opportunities for success suited to the child's capabilities. Opportunities within school do not have to be within the academic realm. It might be that a child develops a sense of self-efficacy through taking the register to the office for the first time or having another special position of responsibility. Through such opportunities the child receives a sense of perceived agency, 'I did it and I can do it again.'

- Take note of what they are good at and build on these achievements. Help pupils to notice and feel good about what they have achieved. Encourage them to use what they have achieved as a way of helping them cope with stress and adversity. Celebrate successes and achievements of all kinds through postcards, exhibitions, assemblies, concerts, certificates etc. Often a thoughtful word to show you have noticed is enough to help them to realise their effort and achievement has not gone unnoticed and will help them to recognise it more themselves. This is in line with 'growth mindset' (see chapter 4 on self-esteem); it is important that you praise their effort rather than their ability. 'You really worked hard at that piece of writing; that must have taken you hours of work!' rather than, 'You are really good at writing.'

- Using a gratitude journal, getting the young person to record three things they are grateful for each day, is an effective way to foster optimism and hope.

Summary

Resilience, as mentioned at the start of the chapter, is a complex issue and we need to be careful in our assessments about who is coping and doing well. Many children and young people are adept at appearing to be coping well with adversity when in fact they may be internalising their symptoms and not coping well at all. We know that it is often a surprise when young people commit suicide, or you find out that someone you thought of as being 'just fine' turns out to have an eating disorder or a problem with alcohol. The key is to look at the internal and external protective factors that a young person has and try to increase the quality or quantity of these factors. We can help young people to improve their emotional literacy skills and help them with strategies for managing uncomfortable emotions, even if that is to accept the emotion and that it will pass; all of this is valuable learning. We should not assume that once a person has been through a difficult episode and found ways to manage that they will be able to cope perfectly the next time adversity strikes. This is an ongoing journey of learning. We all need reminding of new ways of thinking and being that are healthier.

References

Ahlgren, A., & Johnson, D.W. (1979) Sex differences in the correlates of co-operative and competitive school attitudes. *Developmental Psychology*, 19, 881–8.

Baron-Cohen, S. et al (1997) Do children with autism use the Speaker's Direction of Gaze (SDG) strategy to crack the code of language? *Child Development*, 68, 48–57.

Baron-Cohen, S. (2003) *The Essential Difference*. London: Penguin Books.

Barrett, W. and Randall, R. (2004) Investigating the circles of friends approach: Adaptations and implications for practice. *Educational Psychology in Practice*, 20, 4, 353–368.

Baumeister, R. (2005) Rejected and alone. *The Psychologist*, 18, 12, 732–735.

Beesdo, K., Knappe, S. and Pine, D.S. (2009) Anxiety and anxiety disorders in children and adolescents: developmental issues and implications for DSM-V. *The Psychiatric Clinics of North America*, 32, 3, 483–524.

Benson, H. (2010) Family breakdown in the UK: it's not about divorce. Joint report by Bristol Community Family Trust and the Centre for Social Justice.

Bettelheim, B. (1975) *The Uses of Enchantment: The Meaning and Importance of Fairy Tales*. London: Thames & Hudson.

Blair, C. and Raver, C.C. (2012) Individual development and evolution: Experiential canalization of self-regulation. *Developmental Psychology*, 48, 647–657.

Bomber, L.M. and Hughes, D.A. (2013) *Settling to Learn*. London: Worth Publishing.

Borba, M. (1989) *Esteem Builders: A K-8 Self-esteem Curriculum for Improving Student Achievement, Behavior and School Climate*. Fawnskin, CA: Jalmar Press.

Bravery, K. and Harris, L. (2009) Emotional Literacy Support Assistants in Bournemouth: Impact and Outcomes, unpublished doctoral research cited on www.elsanetwork.org/research.

Breakwell, G. (1997) *Coping with Aggressive Behaviour*. Chichester: John Wiley & Sons.

Brett, D. (1986) *Annie Stories*. New York: Workman Publishing.

Brett, D. (1992) *More Annie Stories*. New York: Magination Press.

Buccino, G., Riggio, L., Melli, G. and Al, E. (2005) Listening to action-related sentences modulates the activity of the motor system: A combined TMS and behavioural study. *Cognitive Brain Research*, 24, 355 –363.

Burton, S. and Shotton, G. (2004) Building Emotional Resilience. *Special Children*, 162, September/October, 18–20.

Burton, S., Osborne, C. and Norgate, R. (2010) An evaluation of the impact of the Emotional Literacy Support Assistant project on pupils attending schools in Bridgend, Hampshire. Educational Psychology Service Research and Evaluation Unit, accessed via www.elsanetwork. org/research.

Carlson, S.M., White, R.E. and Davis-Unger, A. (2014) Evidence for a relation between executive function and pretense representation in preschool children. *Cognitive Development*, 29, 1–16.

Chaplin, T. and Aldao, A. (2013) Gender differences in emotion expression in children: A meta-analytic review. *Psychological Bulletin*, 139, 4, 735–765.

Chapman, G. and Campbell, R. (2012) *The 5 Love Languages of Children*. Chicago, IL: Northfield Publishing.

Coie, J.D. and Kupersmidt, J.B. (1983) A behavioral analysis of emerging social status in boys' groups. *Child Development*, 54, 6, 1400–1416.

Connellan, J., Baron-Cohen, S., Wheelwright, S., Batki, A., and Ahluwalia, J. (2001) Sex differences in human neonatal social perception. *Infant Behaviour Development*, 23, 113–118.

Cowen, E.L., Pederson, A., Babigian, H., Izzo, L.D., and Trost, M.A. (1973) Long term follow up of early detected vulnerable children, cited in Frederickson, N. (1991) Helping the rejected child. In Lindsay, G. and Miller, A. (eds.) *Psychological Services for Schools*. Harlow: Longman.

Cresswell, C. and Willetts, L. (2007) *Overcoming Your Child's Fears and Worries*. London: Robinson.

Crick, N.R. and Grotpeter, J.K. (1995) Relational aggression, gender and social-psychological adjustment. *Child Development*, 66, 710–722.

Daniel, B. and Wassell, S. (2002) *The School Years: Assessing and Promoting Resilience in Vulnerable Children 2*. London: Jessica Kingsley.

Deci, E.L. and Ryan, R.M. (2009) The what and why of goal pursuits. *Psychological Inquiry*, 11, 4, 227–268.

Djikic, M. and Oatley, K. (2014) The art in fiction: From indirect communication to changes of the self. *Psychology of Aesthetics, Creativity and the Arts*, 8, 4, 498–505.

Dunn, J. and Deater-Deckard, K. (2001) *Children's Views of Their Changing Families*. York: Joseph Rowntree Foundation.

Dweck, C. (2012) *Mindset: How You Can Fulfil Your Potential*. London: Constable & Robinson.

Dwivedi, K.N. (Ed.) (1997) *The Therapeutic Use of Stories*. London: Routledge.

Fahlberg, V. (1991) *A Child's Journey through Placement*. London: BAAF.

Faupel, A., Herrick, E., and Sharp, P.M. (1998) *Anger Management: A Practical Guide for Teachers*. London: David Fulton.

Fonagy, P., Steele, P., Steele, H., Higgitt, A. and Target, M. (1994) The theory and practice of resilience. *Journal of Child Psychology and Psychiatry*, 35, 231–257.

Frankl, V.E. (1959) *Man's Search for Meaning*. Boston, MA: Beacon Press, 2006.

Frederickson, N. (1991) Helping the rejected child, chapter 8 in Lindsay, G. and Miller, A (eds.) *Psychological Services for Schools*. Harlow: Longman.

Frederickson, N., Warren, L. and Turner, J. (2005) Circle of friends – an exploration of impact over time. *Educational Psychology in Practice*, 21, 3, 197–210.

FRIENDS programmes – http://www.pathwayshrc.com.au/.

Gerhardt, S. (2004) *Why Love Matters: How Affection Shapes a Baby's Brain*. Hove: Brunner-Routledge.

Gilbert, S. (2004) *Grief Encounter*. London: NCB Publications.

Gilligan, R. (2001) *Promoting Resilience*. London: British Agencies for Adoption and Fostering.

Glasser, W. (1998) *Choice Theory: A New Psychology of Personal Freedom.* New York: Harper Perennial.

Glenberg, A.M., Satao, M. and Cattaneo, L. (2008) Processing abstract language modulates motor system activity. *Quarterly Journal of Experimental Psychology*, 61, 905–919.

Goleman, D. (1995) *Emotional Intelligence.* London: Bloomsbury.

Grahamslaw, L. (2010) What is the impact of an ELSA Project on support assistants' and children's self-efficacy beliefs? Unpublished doctoral research cited on www.elsanetwork.org/research.

Gray, C. (2015) *The New Social Story Book.* Arlington, TX: Future Horizons.

Hagerty, B.M. and Williams R.A. (1999) The effects of sense of belonging, social support, conflict, and loneliness on depression. *Nursing Research*, 48, 4, 215–219.

Haidt, J. (2006) *The Happiness Hypothesis.* New York: Basic Books.

Hall, J.A. (1978) Gender effects in decoding nonverbal cues. *Psychological Bulletin*, 85, 845–858.

Harrison, L. and Harrington, R. (2001) Adolescents' bereavement experiences. Prevalence, association with depressive symptoms, and use of services. *Journal of Adolescence*, 24, 2, 159–169.

Hawn Foundation (2011) *The MindUp Curriculum.* New York: Scholastic.

Hill, M., Stafford, A., Seaman, P., Ross, N. and Daniel, B. (2007) *Parenting and Resilience.* York: Joseph Rowntree Foundation.

Hills, R. (2016) An evaluation of the emotional literacy support assistant (ELSA) project from the perspective of primary school children. *Educational and Child Psychology*, 33, 4.

Hoffman, M.L. (1977) Sex differences in empathy and related behaviours. *Psychological Bulletin,* 84, 712–722.

Howe, D. (2005) *Child Abuse and Neglect: Attachment Development and Intervention.* Basingstoke: Palgrave Macmillan.

Huebner, D. and Matthews, B. (2005) *What to Do When You Worry Too Much: A Kid's Guide to Overcoming Anxiety*. Washington, DC: Magination Press.

Hutchings, S., Comins, J. and Offiler, J. (1991) *The Social Skills Handbook*. Bicester: Winslow Press.

Illsley Clarke, J. (1998) *Self-Esteem: A Family Affair*. Center City, MN: Hazelden.

Jackson, S. and Martin, P. (1998) Surviving the care system: education and resilience. *Journal of Adolescence*, 21, 569–583.

Johnson, D.R. (2012) Transportation into a story increases empathy, prosocial behaviour and perceptual bias toward fearful experiences. *Personality and Individual Differences*, 52, 150–155.

Johnson, D.R. (2013) Transportation into literary fiction reduces prejudice against and increases empathy for Arab Muslims. *Scientific Study of Literature*, 3, 77–92.

Kidd, D.C., and Castano, E. (2013) Reading literary fiction improves theory of mind. *Science*, 342, 377–380.

Kircanski, K., Lieberman, M.D. and Craske, M.G. (2012) Feelings into words: contributions of language to exposure therapy. *Psychological Science*, 23, 10, 1086–1091.

Kog, M., and Moons, J. (2008) *A Box Full of Feelings*. Oxford: Speechmark.

LeGoff, D. (2017) *How LEGO-Based Therapy for Autism Works: Landing on My Planet.* London: Jessica Kingsley.

Lieberman, M.D., Eisenberger, N.I., Crockett, M.J., Tom, S.T., Pfeifer, J.H. and Way, B.M. (2007) Putting feelings into words. *Psychological Science*, 18, 5421–428.

Losel, F. and Farrington D.P. (2012) Direct protective and buffering protective factors in the development of youth violence. *American Journal of Preventive Medicine*, 43, 8–23.

Mann, F. and Russell, C. (2011) The impact of ELSA interventions on children and young people. Accessed via www.elsanetwork.org/research.

Mar, R.A., Oatley, K. and Peterson, J.B. (2009) Exploring the link between reading fiction and empathy: Ruling out individual differences and examining outcomes. *Communications: The European Journal of Communications*, 34, 407–428.

Marshmallow Study Revisited, The. New York: University of Rochester, October 11, 2012.

Maslow, A.H. (1943) A theory of human motivation. *Psychological Review,* 50, 370–396.

Maslow, A.H. and Lowery, R. (Eds.) (1998). *Towards a Psychology of Being* (3rd ed.). New York: John Wiley & Sons.

Masten, A, (2014) *Ordinary Magic: Resilience in Development*. London: Guilford Press.

McNamara, E. (1998) *Motivational Interviewing*. Merseyside: Positive Behaviour Management.

Mischel, W., Ebbesen, E. and Raskoff, Z.A. (1972). Cognitive and attentional mechanisms in delay of gratification. *Journal of Personality and Social Psychology,* 21, 2: 204–209.

Monroe, B. and Kraus, F. (2009) *Brief Interventions with Bereaved Children*. Oxford: Oxford University Press.

Newton, C., Taylor, G. and Wilson, D. (1996) Circles of friends: An inclusive approach to meeting emotional and behavioural needs. *Educational Psychology in Practice*, 11, 41–48.

O'Connor, E. (2016) The Use of 'Circle of Friends' strategy to improve social interactions and social acceptance: a case study of a child with Aspergers syndrome and other associated needs. *Support for Learning*, 31, 138–147.

Oram, H. (2008) *Angry Arthur*. London: Andersen Press.

Pearpoint, J., Forest, M. and Snow, J. (1992) *The Inclusion Papers, Strategies to Make Inclusion Work*. Toronto, Canada: Inclusion Press.

Perry, B.D. (2000) Traumatized children: how childhood trauma influences brain development. *Journal of California Alliance for the Mentally Ill*, 11, 1, 48–51.

Peters, S. (2008) *The Chimp Paradox: The Mind Management Programme to Help You Achieve Success, Confidence and Happiness*. London: Vermilion.

Prochaska, J.O. and DiClemente, C.C. (1982) *The Transtheoretical Approach: Crossing Traditional Boundaries of Therapy*. Homewood, IL: Dow Jones-Irwin.

Quinton, D. and Rutter, M. (1988) *Parenting Breakdown: The Making and Breaking of Inter-generational Links*. Aldershot: Avebury.

Rae, T. (1998) *Dealing with Feeling, an Emotional Literacy Curriculum*. Bristol: Lucky Duck Publishing.

Rees, I. (2005) Solution Orientated Work. Training course delivered to Northumberland Educational Psychology Service, Summer 2005.

Robson, C. (2000) *Real World Research*. London: John Wiley & Sons.

Romans, S., Martin, J., Anderson, J., O'Shea, M. and Mullen, P. (1995) Factors that mediate between child sexual abuse and adult psychological outcome. *Psychological Medicine*, 25, 127–142.

Rutter, M. (1999) Resilience concepts and findings: implications for family therapy. *Journal of Family Therapy*, 21, 119–144.

Salovey, P. and Mayer, J.D. (1990). Emotional intelligence. *Imagination, Cognition and Personality*, 9, 185–211.

Schutz, W. (1988) The interpersonal world. In Adler, R.B. and Rodman, G. (Eds.) *Understanding Human Communication* (3rd edn). London: Holt, Rinehart & Winston.

Seiler, L. (2008) *Cool Connections with Cognitive Behavioural Therapy*. London: Jessica Kingsley.

Sharp, P. (2001) *Nurturing Emotional Literacy*. London: David Fulton.

Shotton, G. (1998) A circle of friends approach for socially neglected children. *Educational Psychology in Practice*, 14, 22–25.

Shotton, G. (2002) *The Feelings Diary*. Bristol: Lucky Duck Publishing.

Smith, C. (2016) *Writing and Developing Social Stories*. Milton Keynes: Speechmark.

Stallard, P. (2003) *Think Good – Feel Good*. Chichester: John Wiley & Sons.

Street, S. and Isaacs, M. (1998). Self-esteem: Justifying its existence. *Professional School Counseling*, 1, 3, 46–50.

Sunderland, M. (1993) *Draw on Your Emotions*. Bicester: Speechmark Publishing.

Tannen, D. (1990) *You Just Don't Understand: Women and Men in Conversation*. New York: William Morrow & Co.

Teicher, M. and Sanson, J. (2016) Annual research review: Enduring neurobiological effects of childhood abuse and neglect. *Journal of Child Psychology and Psychiatry*, 57, 3, 241–266.

Tonkin, L. (1996) Growing around grief—another way of looking at grief and recovery. *Bereavement Care Journal*, 15, 1.

Veeken, J. (2012) *The Bear Cards Feelings*. North Bendigo, Australia: Q Cards.

Waddell, M. (1994) *Owl Babies*. London: Walker Books.

Whitaker, P., Barratt, P., Joy, H., Potter, M. and Thomas, G. (1998) Children with autism and peer group support using circle of friends. *British Journal of Special Education*, 25, 60–64.

Wilson, P. and Long, I. (2009) *The Big Book of Blobs*. London: Speechmark.

Wolfe, A., Macfarlane, A., Donkin, A., Marmot, M. and Viner, R. (2014) *Why Children Die: Death in Infants, Children, and Young People in the UK*. London: Royal College of Paediatrics and Child Health and National Children's Bureau.

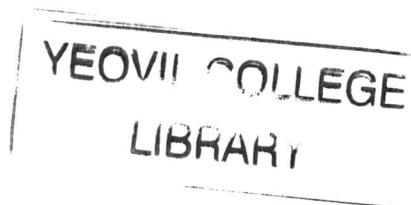